# ACING MOTHERHOOD FAILING MARRIAGE

*15 1/2 Reasons Why I'm Naturally A Better Mom Than Wife And What I'm Doing About It!*

MIRA ROLLINS

Unless otherwise indicated, all Scripture quotations are from The Holy Bible, New International Version, NIV. Copyright 1973, 1978, 1984, 2011 by Biblica, Inc. Used by permission. All rights reserved worldwide.

All the incidents described in this book are true. Where individuals are identified by name, they have granted the author and the publisher the right to use their names, comments, stories and/or facts of their lives in all manners, including composite or altered representations.

Cover Design By: Allyson Rhodes, AIR Designs

Interior Layout By: The Killion Group, Inc

Editing: Karen Rodgers, Critique Editing Services

Acing Motherhood. Failing Marriage.

Copyright 2016 by Mira Rollins.

Published by She Writes for Him Publishers

ISBN 13: 978-0692678862

ISBN 10: 0692678867

Dallas, TX 75104

All rights reserved. No part of this publication may be reproduced, stored in a retrieval system, or transmitted in any form or by any means – electronic, mechanical, digital, photography, recording, or any other – except for brief quotations in printed reviews, without the expressed written permission of the published.

Printed in the United States of America

*To My Lab Partner and Lover Eric,*

*Thanks. Sorry. You're Welcome. I forgive you.
Let's do it all over again tomorrow and forever!*


*To Sincere Wives Everywhere,*

*God knows your heart and sees your effort. I promise!*

# CONTENTS

The PV 31 Pest ..................................................................................... 1
Acknowledgements ............................................................................. 5
Commitments ...................................................................................... 9
CHAPTER 1: You make me feel like a natural woman ................ 15
CHAPTER 2: Man Up .......................................................................... 27
CHAPTER 3: Super Mom! Coming to a theater near you ............. 37
CHAPTER 4: Two Good Hands ........................................................ 45
CHAPTER 5: The Mini Me's have it ................................................. 55
CHAPTER 6: He's not the same man I married ............................. 67
CHAPTER 7: Amnesia Vs Post Traumatic Stress Disorder (PTSD) .... 77
CHAPTER 8: Who's the Boss? .......................................................... 87
CHAPTER 9: Facebook Fairy Tales .................................................. 103
CHAPTER 10: I look better in 3D ..................................................... 111
CHAPTER 11: Enough brownie points should earn brownies ....... 117
CHAPTER 12: Pump Him Up ............................................................ 125
CHAPTER 13: Till Death (or something like it) Do Us Part .......... 139
CHAPTER 14: Fishing, Football, and Fried Food .......................... 145
CHAPTER 15 AND 1/2: Satan is a Hater ........................................ 157
Conclusion ........................................................................................... 165

## *The PV 31 Pest*

I have a top ten list of who I want to meet as soon as I get to heaven. The first few names on the list are likely similar to anyone else's. Of course, the three front runners are God, Jesus, and the Holy Spirit. Next are my relatives who passed on before me, especially my Granny. However, it's around number six or seven when my list looks a little different than most. Right after I marvel at the greatness of God, kiss the nail holes in Jesus' hands, high five the Holy Spirit and get my long missed kiss on the forehead from my granny, I'm looking for Eve and the Proverbs 31 woman. The angels can wait. I will talk to Paul later. More than anything else, I want to have a conversation with those two chicks.

I am looking for Eve to make sure she fully understands the gravity of the drama she caused women over the years with PMS and labor pains. Not even a caramel apple covered in nuts was worth the difficulties that one lethal bite caused.

However, the one person I am looking for with the greatest intensity is Mrs. Goody Two-Shoes. I will fling open every pearly gate and march with my hands on my hips down every gold-paved street looking for Mrs. Proverbs 31. Why? It is because she has created this standard that I have been chasing my entire adult life. It's like always being compared to your older, more mature and perfect sister. Or always standing in the shadow of your older cousin who is a straight-A student, captain of the cheerleading squad, who also won homecoming queen while she simultaneously held down a part-time job.

The PV 31 woman has the following attributes:

- ☐ Her husband thinks she's great. "Her husband has full confidence in her and lacks nothing of value. She brings him good, not harm, all the days of her life" (Proverbs 31:11-12).

- ☐ Her kids love her. "Her children arise and call her blessed" (Proverbs 31:28).

- ☐ She makes tons of money as an entrepreneur. "She considers a field and buys it; out of her earnings she plants a vineyard" (Proverbs 31:16).

  "She makes linen garments and sells them, and supplies the merchants with sashes" (Proverbs 31:24).

- ☐ Her house is well organized. "She watches over the affairs of her household and does not eat the bread of idleness" (Proverbs 31:27).

- ☐ She does ministry work. "She opens her arms to the poor and extends her hands to the needy" (Proverbs 31:20).

- ☐ She has a great attitude and strong confidence as she does it all. "She is clothed with strength and dignity. She can laugh at the days to come" (Proverbs 31:25).

Every time I read that chapter in scripture, I roll my eyes. When she is the topic of another pastor's sermon, I think about leaving church to go buy coffee and donuts. Every time I hear anyone speak about her I feel like a teenager being lectured. If I am honest, it's because I'm jealous.

In all my years of marriage, I have been struggling to achieve her perfect balance of business woman, community contributor, wife and mother. Despite systems learned from books, advice shared from other women, and attending countless women's conferences, I still fall miserably short of the bar she set. If it wasn't for her, I would argue this balance doesn't exist. If not for her, I would confidently argue that the excellent life she led is impossible.

However, I must face the truth because she is written about in the pages of the infallible word of God. The truth is I can no longer put her in the same category as the Abominable Snowman, Martians and

Santa Claus. Unlike them, she is real and she exists. Her existence demands that I seek her excellence. The truth is I have the capacity and responsibility to live a life as consistently honorable as the PV 31 woman.

Once I finally accepted that I should be working towards PV 31 status, I took a self-assessment. In the business woman category, I excelled. As an occupational therapist and manager of multiple therapy clinics, I have had great success over the course of my career. Patients, families, coworkers and employees have all validated my success in various areas of my career. Career, *check*.

Second category, motherhood. My oldest son is one of the smartest and most respectful young men you will ever meet. My middle child and second son is sociable, smart and loveable. My baby and only girl is soaking up life like a sponge and laughs as much as she breaths. They all have areas where there is room for growth, but overall they each are great human beings that I am immensely proud to call mine. I see loving, God fearing, professional adults in the making. Motherhood, *check*.

The final category, helpmate/wife. Um, well, you see, what had happened was, are you asking about today or yesterday; before I answer that question let me explain… When I have to grade myself on my role as a wife, I feel as though I need to defend myself and explain my short falls. Why? The truth is I am a much better mom than I am a wife.

Since you are reading this book, my assumption is that you are as well. So let's unpack this baggage to see why and what we can do about it. Before we begin unpacking, let's make a few acknowledgements and commitments. These acknowledgements will increase our awareness and humility, which will allow us to better receive critique. The commitments will increase our accountability and consistency. The combination of receptivity of personal opportunity areas and consistency in implementing new strategies is the key to creating lasting change. So let's get started changing!

# *Acknowledgements*

Acknowledgement #1: I am responsible for some of the issues in the current state of my marriage. Translation: I made some of this mess.

This book assumes your husband has faults and acknowledges he is not blameless. He actually has a greater accountability than you. Tony Evans in his book *For Married Women Only* says "the primary responsibility for the health of a marriage falls on the husband, not on the wife."

This book, though, is not about him. It's about you. At times it may feel as if I am "letting him off the hook" or "putting all the blame on you." Fight the urge to scream out "What about him?" I am placing strategic laser focus on us, the wives. Whenever you feel as if I am picking on you and ignoring him, I most likely am, purposely. There will be other opportunities, other conferences, and books that put husbands on the hot seat, but not this one. So look at yourself in the mirror and agree to focus on your role in the areas of opportunity in your marriage.

Matthew 7:5 cautions us to "First get rid of the log in your own eye; then you will see well enough to deal with the speck in your friend's eye." The goal is not to ignore the speck, but to first concentrate on the log. I know some of you think you are the speck and he is the log! Whatever the size of the issue, focus solely on yours for now.

I often tell my employees when they get frustrated about someone else's poor performance and the impact it has on their own job, that they must "control the controllables." This simply means that though there are other people and factors that affect the situation, they should only put time, energy and effort into those things they have the ability to change. As we journey through this book, we are only focusing on what we can control. Us!

Another way to look at it is by what my son's pre-kindergarten teacher often told her students. Whenever they would run to her to report what ill another student had done, she would stop them mid-sentence and say "Stop! Tell on yourself first." This book is about telling on ourselves first, fixing those things, so we can then go to God with a clear conscience when it is time to ask for reproof of our husbands.

Say this out loud: I acknowledge that my husband is not solely responsible for the current state of our marriage. I acknowledge and accept responsibility for the areas of struggle in our relationship that were caused by my _____ (fill in the blank, i.e. selfishness, anger, infidelity, etc.) I will now focus my time, energy and effort on addressing those issues.

Acknowledgement #2: I have the ability to improve the current state of my marriage without my husband's participation. Translation: I may have to be the "bigger person" in order for our relationship to improve.

Our society has convinced us that the golden rule of the bible ("Do unto others as you would have them do unto you." Matthew 7:12) promotes weakness and naivety. The fear of being a weak woman who is taken advantage of prevents us from doing what we know in our hearts is right. This fear causes us to live by our own rules. Rules like "if he is going to act like a jerk, then so will I" or "two can play that game" or "I'm not doing this until he does that."

We also fear that if we consistently respond well to our husband's negative behavior, then he will never "get it." It seems as if our good behavior in response to his negative behavior, will allow him to miss his wrong.

Years ago a co-worker gave me marriage advice. I was only married about a year and she felt she had one pearl of wisdom to give me. She looked me straight in my eyes and very sternly said, "Every so often, every man needs to be told off real good. They need it. If not, they will just run all over you." I am ashamed to admit that for a time

I believed that! Needless to say, it did not work for either of us. She is divorced and I spent most of my early years of marriage in an awful power struggle.

Despite what the world has told us, we must choose to believe the word of God that says we can win our husbands over by our gentle and respectful behavior (1 Peter 3:1).

As wives, many times it can feel as if we are putting forth the greatest effort, making the biggest sacrifices, and biting our lip the hardest. What is most frustrating is the feeling of taking the lead in an area that our husbands should be leading. We then become frustrated and stop behaving the way we should.

Consider this. If you are working on a ship that is headed straight towards an iceberg, would you wait on the captain to steer the ship to safety, or would you do what needs to be done to keep the ship from sinking? Hopefully you would take action regardless of the captain's behavior. Many of our marriages are sinking, partially because of our stubborn unwillingness to act. Ladies, don't be stubborn. Grab the wheel and begin steering your marriages to safety. Regardless of what your husband is doing or not doing.

Say this out loud:

- ☐ I acknowledge and accept the call to change. I will not wait on my husband to do so.

- ☐ His behavior will not dictate mine.

- ☐ I will act according to what God says and not what my husband does.

- ☐ I will not be governed by my husband's transgressions against me but by God's expectations of me.

# *Commitments*

Commitment #1: Consistency. Once you identify an area you need to work on to improve your relationship with your husband, keep it up *forever*. Often when we hear an inspiring message at church, get energized during a retreat or read a wonderful new concept in a book, it energizes us. We are excited to put what we learned into practice. However, that spiritual and emotional high deflates like a balloon when met by opposition to our efforts. When the results we hope for don't come, we stop implementing what we committed to.

I implore you to make the concepts from this and all other Godly counsel more than a spiritual high but a spiritual habit.

Say this out loud: No matter how frustrated, tired, disregarded, angry or unappreciated I feel, I will apply wise and spiritual concepts consistently in my relationship with my husband.

Commitment #2: Honesty. Be honest with yourself about areas where you have fallen short. Ask God to help you properly *self-assess*.

Unlike most students, I hated when the teacher allowed us to grade our own papers. The temptation to ignore my incorrect answers or give partial credit was just too much for me. In our marriages, we have to grade our own papers and use the bible as the master key. We have to resist the urge to grade ourselves on a curve and with leniency.

Doing my own taxes is also a struggle. Not because of the mechanics of actually completing them, but because this is another area where I am faced with "telling on myself" and "self-reporting." Though the temptation is great, maturity and integrity say I must correctly self-report on my taxes and in marriage.

We have to be honest with our husbands as various areas of improvement are revealed to us. Ask God to give you the integrity and vulnerability to self-report or confess. As spiritually mature wives, we have to confess our sins to our husbands as God reveals them to us. James 5:16 encourages us to "confess your sins to each other and pray for each other so that you may be healed."

Say this out loud: I will be honest with myself and my husband, no matter how much I dislike the truth. I will trade my desire to be right and the desire to win, for the need to be honest.

Now that you have acknowledged your role, your power and your commitment to consistency and honesty, you are ready to dive in. This dive takes you deep, but there is treasure to be found.

*The 3 Ps*

At the end of each chapter you will see points to ponder, pray for and practice. These are crucial steps to experiencing the effectiveness of this book. If you read it like a novel instead of a workbook, the likelihood of real change is slim. Take the time after every chapter to…

Ponder

- Reflect on the principle.
- Remember a situation that applies.
- Relive an encounter.
- Relate to the example. This step makes it relevant.

Ask yourself questions such as "What could I have said differently? "What was I feeling that made me react that way?" "How can I practically and immediately apply this principle to my situation?"

When I attended my oldest son's induction into the National Jr Honor society, the president of the organization read aloud the induction pledge. The inductees were to repeat each portion after her. The first sentence of the pledge was "I \_\_\_\_\_, promise to uphold…"

*Acing Motherhood But Failing Marriage*

The president put her name in the blank and figured the inductees would understand they should replace her name with each of their own individual names. They didn't. Instead, each of the 25 "smart kids" repeated the president's name. After lots of laughter from the students and audience, she explained what she wanted them to do. They got it straight the second time around.

How about you? When you read this and other books, are you putting others' names in the blanks and not inserting your own where needed? Can you see your friends' and family members' faults clearly; however, struggle to see your own? If you are not honest with yourself about your strengths and weaknesses, then real change will not occur.

Pray – Ask God for an abundance of conviction, discernment, forgiveness, and dedication. We cannot make our marriages work using our own human power. No matter how much you learn about developing a healthy marriage, you must rely on the power of God to apply what you've learned.

I can't tell you the number of times I have read a manual to put something together, learn a new computer system or a recipe to cook a new meal. Though my reading and comprehension skills are pretty good, I never seem to get it just right. Something is either leaning, locked out or burned.

When I call someone for help who has expertise in that area, things start to fall right into place. So it is with prayer. No matter what books you read—including the bible itself—if you don't seek God's wisdom on the subject, you will forever struggle.

Think of good advice, conferences, books and other resources as an unlit match and a log. Now think of prayer as adding gasoline and that now lit match to a dry log. If you want principles you learn to catch on, accelerate and not fizzle out, you must pray. Through prayer, God will give you strength, specific strategy and support.

As we press through the stormy seasons of life we must take courage from the example in Psalm 107:28-30, which states "Then they cried out to the Lord in their trouble, and he brought them out of their distress. He stilled the storm to a whisper; the waves of the sea were hushed. They were glad when it grew calm, and he guided them to their desired haven."

Practice – Application of what you learn brings change. Many of the concepts in this book will not come naturally. Therefore, you must practice them until they become second nature. One of the most widely quoted yet inaccurate life lessons is "Practice makes perfect." Not even the PV 31 woman was perfect. Stop striving for that! The truth is, "Practice makes better." This is the point of the book, to help make you a better—not perfect—wife to your husband.

The only way you get better is to practice. You didn't learn the clarinet, to sing on key, to run a marathon or any other achievement in your life without practice. So don't think that being a great wife is any different. You must practice being full of the "ful" that you want. In order to be respect*ful* and help*ful* and delight*ful*, you must be *full* of those things *before* you need to manifest them. You can't be respectful if you have not practiced respect. If you are only resent*ful*, disrespect*ful*, and spite*ful*, then that is what will spill over because that is what you are *full* of. What are you full of? What are you practicing?

So get ready to ponder, pray, and practice in order to be a better wife. Let's get started.

Disclaimer: Before we dive in, I want to make one clarification. This book is about marriage not motherhood. Please don't mistake that I am saying you should stop or start doing anything differently related to mothering your children. This book uses motherhood as a comparison to marriage in order to highlight the disparities. It is not used to suggest that you should shrink away from those things that make you a great mom. I believe that you can be a great wife and a great mom at the same time.

# FACEBOOK FUNNIES:

Throughout this book you will find snippets from my Facebook posts about my family. Enjoy!

Sitting watching "The age of Adaline" with my husband and he turns to me and says, "He kind of looks like Harrison Ford." Eric Rollins you make me laugh.

— May 21, 2015

# CHAPTER 1

# *You make me feel like a natural woman*

*For the flesh desires what is contrary to the Spirit, and the Spirit what is contrary to the flesh. They are in conflict with one another, so that you are not to do whatever you want. Galatians 5:17*

Sitting next to me as I type is one of my twins. Some of you are flipping to the back cover to re-read my bio and are very confused. Let me hurriedly explain. I have held on to my two Kid Sister dolls, Brianna and Kianna, since I got them Christmas in 1987. At that young age, the thought of being a mommy excited me. So I mimicked what I thought a good mom was with my dolls. I hugged them, kissed them, carried them around everywhere, bathed and dressed them and tucked them in at night. As the years went on, I played with them less and less but I kept them as a reminder that one day I was going to have a real baby of my own. Now as I look at Kianna (yes I know them apart) I get a warm feeling just remembering how long it's been since knowing that I was born to be a mom. The maternal instinct and desire to be a mother has been in me for as long as I can remember. It just always was.

However, I don't remember dreaming about being a wife until much later in life. Honestly, I would say it was around age 25 when I first got a real desire to be married. Of course throughout high school and college I dated and desired relationships, but I never thought seriously about marriage until my mid to late 20s.

Eventually they both came to be. I married and started a family. The first day one of my little ones came home from the hospital, I just knew what to do. I don't remember being afraid that I was going to drop, break or hurt them. I somehow instinctively knew what to do and how to do it. Along the way, I did seek advice from friends and the internet, but for the most part I just did what came naturally. Judging from their smiles, laughter, intact fingers and toes, and lack of major injuries, my natural instinct has worked.

I can't say the same about marriage. The reality of how ill equipped I was slapped me in the face on a beautiful road in Hawaii on our honeymoon. Little arguments about what to eat turned into huge disagreements about selfishness. Differences of opinion about buying souvenirs transformed into battles about finances. Though the majority of our vacation was fabulous, I knew that I was in over my head. Nothing about relating to my husband in a submissive, loving, and helpful way was coming naturally or easily. If I couldn't get it right while surrounded by the beautiful beaches of Hawaii, how was I going to survive when we returned to real life? The answer—not well.

Over the years, both marriage and motherhood have been challenging, but there has been one major difference: Motherhood feels natural even when it's difficult. Marriage, however, feels like trying to run a race backwards, or write with my left hand though I am right handed or eating soup with a fork. It's just not natural.

Why is that? Why is the natural instinct of motherhood present in most women but the ability to be a good help mate is not. This is the question I asked myself one day after a big argument with my husband. To console myself after the disagreement, I picked up my little baby and stroked her hair as she slept and immediately felt as if all was right with the world. The relationship with my child instantly brought me peace and to "my happy place." At that moment, God showed me the problem. He spoke to my spirit, almost in an audible voice, and told me my relationship with my husband and children were dangerously out of balance. I had to figure out how to bring these relationships back into proper proportion in order to create a healthier marriage.

Many of you share this same experience. There is no wrong in being naturally better at motherhood then wifedom. The problem arises when you convince yourself that it is ok. Ladies, it's not ok!

The single most important relationship you have on Earth, above all others, is your relationship with your spouse. It should be held in higher regard than the relationship with your parents, friends and even your children. All of the other relationships serve many Godly purposes, but marriage is the relationship that God specifically set up to show, grow, and so that others may know.

*Show:*

Marriage was designed to show the world an example of God's love towards us. Ephesians 5:23-28 says "For the husband is the head of the wife as Christ is the head of the church, his body, of which he is the Savior. Now as the church submits to Christ, so also wives should submit to their husbands. Husbands, love your wives, just as Christ loved the church and gave himself up for her to make her holy, cleansing her by the washing with water through the word, and to present her to himself as a radiant church, without stain or wrinkle or any other blemish, but holy and blameless. In the same way husbands ought to love wives as their own bodies."

Marriage is the only relationship that God has specifically set as an example of His love for us.

*Grow:*

Marriage is the way that God chose to increase the number of Christ followers on the earth. Genesis 1:28 states that "God blessed them and said to them, 'Be fruitful and increase in number; fill the earth and subdue it.'"

Marriage is the only relationship that God has specifically designated to create life.

So that others may *Know*:

John 13:35 makes it clear that Christians will be identified as authentic Christians by the love they show. Marriage is the most intimate of all relationships which; therefore, can reflect the deepest level of love.

Marriage provides a platform, like no other relationship, to model God's love. Marriage, therefore, can be used to turn others to Christ when effectively and authentically modeled.

Understanding why God placed such a high value on the marriage relationship will prayerfully allow you to do the same. It may be a hard pill to swallow, but simply put, your relationship with your husband should get more time, energy, and effort than any other, even that of your children.

Here is a short quiz to help you determine the balance you have in your relationship with your husband and children.

For each question that you would choose your husband's need/want, write the number 2. For each question that you would choose your child's need/want, write the number 1. Answer instinctively and honestly!

1. Your husband loves to debrief about his day in bed at night. It helps him unwind. You've noticed that on the nights he talks to you about his day, he does not watch as much TV and is able to get to sleep before 11. Your daughter loves to be read to at night. You have noticed that when you read to her she does not consistently get out of the bed asking for water as an excuse not to go to sleep. You are exhausted from a long day and only have energy to do one or the other. Who gets the pillow time?

2. You have been promising your daughter you would have lunch with her at school all year. Your husband has been dropping hints he would love it if you stopped by his office to try out

a new deli nearby. You get an unexpected break in your work day. Who will you choose as your lunch date?

3. You overbooked the family's schedule for Saturday. Your son has been excited about going to his classmate's big party at his favorite amusement park. It is all he has talked about for the past two weeks. You also made plans to go to dinner with your husband's friend who is in town for a rare visit. Does your son get to go to the party or are you joining your husband for dinner?

4. You pick your son up from school and he proudly boasts about his good exam grade. He requests pizza for dinner as a reward. You readily agree. Just then, your husband texts and reminds you to pick up dinner. You and he had a conversation this morning about him craving an old fashioned grilled cheeseburger. You only have time for one stop. Does your son get the dinner of his choice or does your husband?

5. You and your husband have been doing great on budgeting. You squeezed out a few extra bucks this month and are planning on one splurge! Your son got straight A's and has been asking for a new pair of pricey tennis shoes. Your husband wants a specific golf club. Who gets treated this month?

6. When your daughter needs to be rocked to sleep and your husband could use a head rub to get him to sleep faster. Who gets your soothing touch first?

7. Everyone is in the living room. Your husband likes to unwind while watching the news. Your son likes to do the same by watching cartoons. Do you tell your son to go watch TV in his room or ask your husband to go watch the news in the bedroom?

8. Your husband does not like big crowds but your kids love large family events. The party has gone on for several hours. Your

husband gives you the "look" signaling he is ready to leave. Your kids are running around with uncontrollable laughter. Do the kids get an extra 15 minutes of family play time or do you oblige your husband and pack up immediately?

9. You've been away on a business trip for a week. Your husband and daughter are waiting at the airport for you. As you come down the stairs you hear your daughter scream "Mom!" Your husband flashes a smile and blushes when he sees you. Who do you reach to embrace first?

10. Your daughter is having a teenage tantrum because she does not want to go on the family summer vacation. If she goes on vacation, she will miss the opportunity to work at her "dream job." Your husband really wants the entire family to go on vacation. He leaves the decision to you. You can arrange for your daughter to stay with your mother while the rest of the family goes on vacation. Does your daughter get to work or does your husband get to have the whole family together?

Scoring:

20 – 17: You are the Priority Princess. You consistently elevate your husband though it sometimes means disappointing your children. You understand that saying "yes" more to your husband shows him that you respect and consider him. You also understand saying "no" to your children, is not harmful but sets healthy limits.

16 – 12: You are the Tightrope Tinkerbell. You are trying to equally please your husband and your children. You are afraid to disappoint either one of them, so you vacillate between them both. You spend your days trying to make them both happy by walking this delicate balance of "sometimes yes" and "sometimes no." Though you are trying to please them both, you are actually creating frustration, confusion and competition.

11 and under: You are living in Mommy Madness. Your children are steering decisions by tugging too tightly on your heart. You falsely believe to disappoint them is to damage them. You also believe that saying "no" shows you don't love them. Somehow though, you believe saying "no" to your husband, has no bearing on your love or respect for him.

I am sure many of you are rolling your eyes saying, "Of course I would hug my daughter who is screaming my name first, she's a kid. That does not mean I love her more."

I would like to hone in on three words: "of course" and "love." First, saying "of course" shows that you not only feel that it is the natural decision, but it is also the correct decision. However, you must realize that what is natural is not necessarily right. It is often a natural bodily response to burp after drinking soda. Yet you have managed to master refraining from loud public belching. You have mastered the art of conspicuous belching in order to preserve others perception of you. Laughing is a natural inclination when you witness something funny, but you have learned to mask your amusement when someone falls. You resist the urge to laugh out of respect, consideration and concern.

These are but two examples that prove that what comes naturally must often be resisted. The urge to please your children at the expense of your husband is natural but must be resisted. Disclaimer: Please note that I am not suggesting that the physical or emotional wellbeing of your children be neglected for the sake of your husband (or anyone). To be crystal clear, I am stating that the needs and wants of your husband are priority, period.

Another way to think about the word "natural," is to use the word "fleshly." Often the responses that come "naturally" stem from our sin nature. Read below several verses about our flesh.

Colossians 3:5 "Put to death, therefore, whatever belongs to your earthly nature"

Romans 8:5 "Those who live according to the flesh have their minds set on what the flesh desires; but those who live in accordance with the Spirit have their minds set on what the Spirit desires."

Matthew 15:19 "For out of the heart come evil thoughts"

As women, our maternal instinct is natural. In most situations, it is a good thing. It is God given to protect our children. However, within the confines of our marriages, it can be destructive if not properly checked.

A good friend of mine, also a wife, posted these wise words on Facebook one day: "Just a portion of what is wrong with this world is that we first do what feels right instead of doing what is right."

For one quiet moment, will you consider that you may have been doing what feels right in your marriage, though it may not actually be right? Putting our children first over all things feels right. Putting our husband's first over all things feels difficult, humbling, unfair, and makes you feel unappreciated. Yet it is the right thing to do. Resist the natural, the flesh, and do the right thing.

Do not be afraid your children will become insecure if they feel they are not your number one priority. The benefits of having a well nurtured spouse will add security, peace and assurance to your children. Children need to know that the health of mommy and daddy's marriage is the number one priority in your home. They need to know that when mommy and daddy are good, the children will reap healthy benefits.

Matthew 6:33 promises us that if we "seek first his kingdom and his righteousness, all these things will be given to you as well." This verse suggests that there are automatic benefits to having life's priorities straight. This applies to your marriage. Your children will reap automatic and supernatural benefits in a healthy marriage.

The second word that I want to zero in on is "love." The word of God never suggested that you love your husband more than your children. Neither is that what I am suggesting. The bible instructs us not to love our husbands more, but to esteem the relationship higher. Or to place a greater value on. Or to hold in higher regard. Or to place as a greater priority.

It's not an issue of love but an issue of levels. Does your husband or your children rank higher when it comes to your daily decisions? The only right answer is your husband.

Being a mother comes naturally to most women. Being a wife does not. Therefore, we have to be more intentional about being a better wife. Begin to be intentional about esteeming your husband higher. There is nothing "wrong" with you when esteeming your husband is not your first thought, because being a wife is difficult. You will only be "wrong," if you choose to continue to live out your marriage this way.

Ponder:

Recall a specific situation or situations in which you put your children before your husband. What were your reasons for doing so? Did you feel justified or guilty? What message do you think it sent to your children? What message do you think it sent to your husband? Be certain; both received clear messages.

Pray:

Lord, help me to work through the guilt I feel for placing the needs of my husband over my children. Allow me to resist the natural urge to elevate the role of mother over that of wife. Restore the correct balance in these relationships.

Practice:

What are specific healthy boundaries you can set with your children that will properly prioritize your relationships? What specific ways can you demonstrate to your husband that he is the priority in your life?

## FACEBOOK FUNNIES:

(posted by Eric) Why do women have to talk so much after church...just get in the Car already!

— June 1, 2014

CHAPTER 2

## *Man Up*

*Practice these things, immerse yourself in them, so that all may see your progress. 1 Timothy 4:15*

It's just the letter H. It seems so simple to me but not for Yuriah. These simple three straight lines are stumping him and frustrating me. I now hate the letter H. I will never write the words heal, him, or even heaven again. Just before I go over the edge, I remember he is only three and he is learning. That simple reminder restores my patience and my desire to help him. After reminding myself that my child is developing and learning, my tone and attitude change. I realize I shouldn't get upset with him for what he does not know and has not yet perfected.

News flash, our husbands do not know and have not perfected anything. Sorry, that was a typo. I meant they do not know and have not perfected *everything*. Remind yourself of that and see if your attitude and tone change. They should. We must afford our husbands the same space to grow and grace to fail as we do our children.

Our husbands will make mistakes in parenting that seem so simple to us. Give him grace. He will make a financial decision that may negatively affect your household. He's not perfect. Our spouses are still learning, growing and developing. To expect 100% accuracy sets your husband up for failure.

Yes, your grown husband is still growing. Learning is a lifelong process. His height and shoe size may have maxed out around the age of 20 but not his knowledge, intelligence, and experiences. Our husbands need to be treated with just as much sensitively and patience as our children because they too are growing. Each day my son learns a new word. Each day my husband learns a new truth about the world. Every day my daughter becomes more secure in her walking abilities. Each day my husband becomes more secure in his leadership abilities. My understanding of their growth process increases my sensitivity and support.

*English Class or Chemistry Lab*

As women, we often feel men "should just know" things. Can you hear yourself saying to your husband any of the following?

- ☐ "I figured you would know that. I didn't think I had to tell you."
- ☐ "My dad always did that, so I just thought you would, too."
- ☐ "I just assumed you would know that."

Can you see how destructive these words and this attitude could be to a man's ego and a husband's confidence? If you have ever expressed these sentiments, whether in word or actions, understand that you have hurt your husband's pride.

With every word you speak to your husband, you are either building him up or tearing him down. Proverbs 14:1 says, "The wise woman builds her house, but with her own hands *the foolish* one tears hers down." This question will sound harsh, but are you being a fool? Are your careless words consistently eroding the foundation of your home? Are your disrespectful conversations like grenades?

Our understanding and acceptance of the reality of our husbands' growth will allow us to tap into the necessary compassion and patience that we often lack. You will not have to find patience; it will come automatically. So don't be the snooty teacher looking down on him. Be his lab partner, experimenting and learning together.

Think about that example. Remember back to the sternest English teacher you had in school. You were excited to share a poem you wrote for homework the night before. Instead of listening and being interested in your thoughts, she corrected your sentence structure and grammar. You were excited to turn in a book report, but when she returned it to you, it was bleeding with red corrections. She always seemed more interested in correcting you than connecting with you. Does that describe your relationship with your husband? If I asked your husband, would he say that you corrected him or connected with him more?

Now think back to chemistry class—the lab, not the lecture portion. Big protective goggles, white coats, frogs in jars of solution, the smell of chemicals and a table made for two, you and your partner. Together you explored and experimented. No judgment, no pressure, just the unstated but understood agreement to figure things out together. Sometimes coming to the right conclusion other times not. But together, you learned from your successes and your mistakes.

Is the environment you've created for your husband as cold and critiquing as a stern English classroom? Or is it as safe as a high school chemistry lab?

Here are four of my own examples of being correcting and connecting.

English Teacher Moment (critiquing and correcting)

- ☐ My husband was working for a company he loved but in a position he didn't and with a boss he loved even less. As the days and weeks went by, his frustration in this role mounted. He would share stories with me of how difficult the position was and the lack of support he got from his supervisor. One night after working on a major project for hours, he came into the bedroom to let off steam. As he vented, his voice rose. Not at me, just in general. In the middle of his rant I interrupted him to tell him he was being rude and abrasive in his speech. I told him that even though he was frustrated, there was a proper way to vent. In utter disbelief, he turned and walked out of the room. At that moment, I stood self-righteous, feeling as though I was right to correct him. Now looking back, I see that instead of offering a listening ear and supportive spirit, I chastised him and completely missed the opportunity to connect.

☐ I went out with a group of my girlfriends one night and Eric agreed to stay at home with our children. I got back after 10 p.m. expecting the kids to be long since in bed. Instead I not only found them wide awake, but laying on the couch with Eric watching "Lizard Lick" and eating popcorn. I immediately went into the fact that they should have been sleeping, the show was not appropriate and it was too late to be eating. Never once in that moment did it dawn on me that the sight of my children cuddled underneath their dad was beautiful. None of them had to take the SAT the next morning, so why was being in bed so crucial? "Lizard Lick" is a show about cars being towed, not murder, sex or scandal. Not quite "Mickey Mouse Clubhouse" but far from the X-rated movie my reaction would have indicated. And snacking after dinner, I still can't remember why I had an issue with that. Instead of allowing him to figure out his own routine with the kids and being appreciative that I had a night away, I went into critique mode.

Lab Partner Moment (connecting):

☐ My husband and I once owned a soft serve frozen yogurt shop. This was our first real stab at entrepreneurship. There is so much to learn, it can be overwhelming. He was spearheading the effort and I played the role of co-owner and assistant manager. After successfully executing most of the steps of opening a new business, he forgot a couple. One being to correctly transfer the electricity in our name. On our second day of ownership we came into a hot dark shop. All of our yogurt and cold toppings were spoiled and had to be discarded. We turned loads of customers away. We were on the phone all day trying to get the problem corrected asap. This was a significant mistake and an even bigger hassle. But I didn't say "How could you miss this one? Electricity, really? Of all the things you could have gotten wrong, why this one?" I focused on the fact that he had remembered 1000 other things and that this was his first time ever doing this and he was still learning. I jumped right in and helped him do everything that needed to be done without accusations or finger pointing.

- ☐ Over the years my husband has taken on several home improvement projects, each having varying levels of success. With the projects that left much to be desired, I didn't nitpick about the imperfect edges or express my desire to get it professionally done. I picked up a hammer or a brush and got to work alongside him. We've become amateur carpenters, having fun, bonding and connecting while we work.

*Take Yourself Off the Pedestal*

Our lack of humility can also make us overly critical of our husbands. Many times we give ourselves grace and make allowances for ourselves that we do not give our spouses. If we forget to pay a bill we realize it is because we had so many other things to do, so forgetting one thing is understandable. If we have an abnormally short fuse it should be permissible because of the stress we are under, balancing work and home.

However, we do not give our husbands those allowances during times when they show the slightest imperfection. This can create a pattern of excuses for ourselves yet strict judgment of our husbands.

Read the following verses and see if you find yourself anywhere between these lines.

- ☐ Proverbs 26:12 "Do you see a man who is wise in his own eyes? There is more hope for a fool than for him."

- ☐ Isaiah 5:21 "Woe to those who are wise in their own eyes, and shrewd in their own sight!"

- ☐ Philippians 2:3 "But in humility, consider others better than yourselves."

- ☐ Romans 2:1-4 "So when you, a mere human being, pass judgment on them and yet do the same things, do you think you will escape God's judgment?"

We must be careful that we do not become judgmental toward our spouses. Understand that there are many situations that you too are "learning on the job." As you desire patience, support and encouragement in these situations, so do they.

Being hypercritical in this manner is not only poison to your marriage but sin before God. And wherever there is sin, death follows. If your husband feels you are a snooty, stern and hypercritical teacher, looking over the top of your reading glasses, then he will distance himself from you emotionally and physically. The health of your relationship will be compromised. The destruction and death of your marriage will be near.

It is imperative that you do not make him feel as if he lacks intelligence or belittle him about things he doesn't know. You must have an attitude that says "I support you as you learn and I do not judge you for what you don't know." If he "trusts" that he is safe to explore and grow, he will perfect things at an accelerated rate. So if you want a more intelligent husband, become a more supportive and encouraging wife.

Jada Edwards, a bible teacher and pastor's wife in Dallas, encourages wives to treat their husbands like the men they want them to be, not necessarily the men they are. When we take this approach, they will eventually rise to your level of expectation. Call him higher by your treatment of him! Begin to treat your husband as if he is the most intelligent, handy, funny and mature man you know. Then stand back and watch him morph.

## Faster and Better

When my son was around the age of 4, getting him ready was no easy feat. What should have been a relatively quick and simple process, would normally turn into a frustrating and unnecessarily long project. Why? Because he wanted to 'do it by myself.' And also because he 'knew how.'

He could button his own shirt, or so he said. Somehow he ignored the fact that his small, weak and uncoordinated fingers would drag what should have been a 30 second process out to a 5-minute ordeal. At the end of this drawn out process, he was frustrated, I was irritated and 4 buttons were still left undone.

He would also tell me he could pour his own juice. That is, however, right before he told me he could get his own paper towel to clean the juice from the kitchen floor.

He could brush his own teeth, cut his own meat, unbuckle his own car seat, and about 1000 other things. It never dawned on him that his breath still smelled, his meat was still "choke size" and that I had unloaded all the groceries and the baby while he still struggled with his car seat latch. Sometimes I felt like putting my hands on his face until his lips pooched out, looking him square in his eyes and telling him, **"Let me do it, because I can do it faster and better than you."**

But I didn't! I knew that he would not learn unless he did it on his own. I was also intentional about supporting and protecting his self-esteem. We should take the same measures with our husbands. There will be many situations in our marriages where we can do things faster and better than our husbands. However, we must refrain from and resist the urge to do so.

The more you project yourself as the "expert," the more he will begin to become apathetic to the situation and the outcome. If you always know the best way to do everything, he will begin to stand back and let you do everything. He will become uninterested and disengaged.

You have to decide if being right is more important than your relationship. If efficiency is better than intimacy. And if boosting your ego is more important than uplifting his.

We have all heard that "love is patient." Sometimes the best way you can love your husband is to let him figure it out without jumping in to do it. Have the patience to wait for his light bulb to come on before you come in with your overbearing flood lights.

The moments of intimacy will abound as you sit back and allow him to learn. Whether he states it or not, he will appreciate the respect you show him in this way. So remember, your husband should not be expected to know everything or get everything right. Be his support as he learns and grows.

Ponder:

In what specific situation or area of your husband's life have you been impatient and judgmental because he has not mastered or perfected it?

Pray:

Lord, please supply me with patience, compassion and wisdom to effectively help my husband in [insert the specific area].

Practice:

The next time this area surfaces, ask your husband if there is anything you can do to help. Encourage him verbally in this area.

# FACEBOOK FUNNIES:

I'm tired. Like "I can't move from sitting on this step even though my kids are running around the house" tired. Jesus, give me a second wind, please. Amen and thanks in advance.

— Feb 8, 2013

CHAPTER 3

## *Super Mom! Coming to a theater near you*

*But the greatest among you shall be your servant. And whoever exalts himself shall be humbled; and whoever humbles himself shall be exalted. Matthew 23:11-13*

I thought this kind of stuff only happened in the movies. This would have been a great comedic scene on the big screen, but it was not at all funny when it was happening in my bathroom. I put my then one-year-old in the bathtub, turned to get her towel and what I saw when I turned back around sickened me. She was propped in her poop position. I knew this position very well. Before I could swoop her up, it was done. There were three brown floaties in the water. As I contemplated what to do, I realized that whatever I decided, I had to act fast because the three were separating into many. Without any further thought, I put my bare and ungloved hand in the water and commenced to scoop poop from the tub to the toilet.

After the initial shock and horror, I was fine. I was over it. I'm a mom, that's what I do. I clean poop, suck mucus noses, take rectal temps, stay up late, wake up early, and whatever else is needed to get the job done. I'm a mom.

When I say that, I visualize a picture of me standing in a Superman stance with an "M" on my chest. Now that you have the full picture, I'll say it again: I'm a mom.

Most moms share my sentiment that being a mom is the most prestigious job you can have. It is the highest calling one can aspire to. It is an honor and a privilege to be a mom.

Saying I'm a wife doesn't bring the same heroic feeling. Instead of Superman, the visual I get is Edith Bunker. I'm proud to be Eric's wife and most times I enjoy it. However, when I say Mom and then say Wife, one makes me smile a little bigger and stand a little straighter.

So it's easier for me to use my fingers to remove nose boogies than it is to use those same fingers to pick underwear up from the bathroom floor. I don't resent my children when I have to miss an important personal event on their behalf, but I get angry when the situation happens because of my husband's schedule. The inconveniences and struggles associated with being a mother seldom hit our emotional barometer but those of being a wife boil over quickly. Why? Because, as one of my former bible teachers said, "We behave as we believe."

We believe motherhood is a position of honor, so we act as such. Our belief that being a wife is work, a job, a task, and a chore causes us to behave as such. What would happen if our belief about marriage was elevated?

Let me help you change your beliefs a little bit. The next time you pick underwear up off the bathroom floor, don't think of it as being "a maid for a grown man who should know better" but as just one step in the process of consistently making your home clean, orderly and inviting. No longer think of getting his clothes from the cleaners as "being the underappreciated errand girl," but as the personal assistant to one of the most intelligent business men you know. Don't dread another "download about his job as he talks about people you don't know" but as the sounding board to a strong man, trusting you with his vulnerability.

Each time you are tempted to minimize and diminish your role as a wife, choose to reframe it. People have joked for years about a housewife being a "domestic engineer," but that's exactly the line of thinking that will change your behavior. Give yourself a promotion in your home. You have an important job description as a wife.

In an article from Thebusinessofmarriage.net, Melissa Thoma created this great job description for mothers.

Job Title:

Life Mate, Manager of Spousal Relationships for Family Unit.

Position Posting:

Family unit seeks female senior executive for full-time (we're talking *all* the time) development of intimate relationships, nurture, care and feeding of mate and offspring. This exciting and creative venture seeks to execute a multigenerational strategy of developing the highest possible quality of life through shared resources and support. The very life and happiness of team members will be the responsibility of the Life Mate, who will leverage her skills in communications and negotiation to ensure the health of the primary couple relationship and the proper development of junior staff.

The Life Mate must pledge her permanent fidelity to the enterprise and must be willing to assign all assets and available resources to the job.

Responsibilities include:

- ☐ Willingness to relocate anywhere and everywhere that opportunity may take the business unit
- ☐ Feeding, clothing, housing and primary care of the company and its staff
- ☐ Development and coordination of schedules that accommodate all parties
- ☐ Continuous guidance, mentoring, development, discipline and management of junior staff

Now when you put it that way, that's a pretty important job. So the next time you say that you are a wife, don't think Edith but think Michelle Obama, Jacquelyn Onassis or Lady Bird Johnson. That's right! Elevate yourself to first lady status. Your husband may not be president, but to you, he is just that important (or at least he should be). If he is that important, then that makes your support of him as important as the role of FLOTUS. He can't do it without you.

In addition to being the first lady, you are also his vice president, cabinet member, secret service and press secretary all wrapped in one. As the VP you stand in his stead whenever needed. You are also able to carry out his vision as if he were there himself. As a member of his secret service you move obstacles and barriers from his path, with or without his knowledge. These obstacles would otherwise prevent him from accomplishing the family's goals. As his press secretary, you publically esteem and uplift him so everyone around you knows the great man he is.

Many times it might mean scrubbing the stain out of his white shirt. Other times it might be burning the midnight oil helping him complete a proposal for a major project at work. Support is never small. Encouragement is always important. Being his teammate is never trivial. Your role as a wife, in whatever capacity you are serving at the time, is always a big deal. *You* are a big deal!

No matter the function of the role we are serving in at the time, we must honor our commitment even when it is not cool or convenient. It will not be cool to honor the commitment when your girlfriends are going out but you have to pass up on the opportunity because you agreed to help your husband clean the garage. Not cool, but it's part of your commitment. The commitment won't be convenient when you just found your comfy spot in bed and just began drifting off to sleep but your husband gives you that all too familiar nudge. Not convenient, but part of the commitment.

A good friend and pastor, Daryl Jones, shared this about his wife on Facebook one day:

## Acing Motherhood But Failing Marriage

"Let me do what Proverbs 31:30 says and praise my Proverbs 31:10-31 wife. Yesterday I snagged a pair of shorts on a dresser drawer causing a slight tear. I was getting ready for bible study and was upset. She said take them off. She pulls out a needle and thread. Sews it up real quick and threw it on the bed saying 'Here you go.' This woman is the bomb and is truly a Biblical wife in every way. I thank God for her every day!"

Remember that no matter how seemingly insignificant or of colossal importance, serve him well and willingly. Serving well implies excellence. Serving willingly implies a great attitude. Commit to top-notch service with a smile even when it's not cool or convenient.

Ponder:

What is the most trivial, irritating or minuscule thing you do for your husband that has upset you in the past? How can you reframe your belief regarding it in a more positive way? Why is it important? How does it advance your husband's life?

Pray:

Lord, give me the humility to embrace the areas of marriage that are not flattering, the wisdom to handle those that are grand and the grace to handle both with the same diligence.

Practice:

Ask your husband if there is anything you can do to help him today. Let him know you are willing to help him whatever the task. Let him see the positive attitude you have in doing it. Whatever "it" is.

# FACEBOOK FUNNIES:

OK, so this morning I am getting the littles ready and they are playing and running and screaming. So I calmly say, stop screaming. They continue. So I say a little louder, stop screaming. By the third time my voice is at a yell and I say "stop screaming." Then Yuriah looks at me and says "You too mommy, stop screaming." Lmbo

— Jan 6, 2013

CHAPTER 4

# *Two Good Hands*

*Exercising oversight, not under compulsion, but willingly, as God would have you; not for shameful gain, but eagerly; not domineering over those in your charge, but being examples to the flock.*
1 Peter 5:2-5

Between the 3 of my children, I estimate that I do over 100 things for them each day. These "things" range from tying shoes, scheduling doctors' appointments, cooking, and playing chauffeur. If I don't do them, they won't get done. My babies can't do these things for themselves. Yuriah's fine motor coordination is not developed well enough to tie his shoes. Kaden can't drive yet. Danielle can't use a fork well, let alone cook for herself. So I have to do it. Knowing that they can't do it for themselves makes it natural for me to do it for them, without frustration or resentment.

However, my husband has two strong and coordinated hands. He can use them to clean up, cook, make his own appointments, and do whatever else he needs to do for himself. So when he is lying on the couch and asks me to bring a soda, my mind thinks and sometimes my mouth says, "What's wrong with your hands?" It is more difficult for me to complete paperwork, run an errand or schedule an appointment for my husband because my flesh screams out, "You can do it yourself!"

How about you? Does it irritate you to do the many things for your husband that he is capable of doing on his own? Do you feel taken advantage of when you add a task to your already lengthy to-do list that he does not need your help with but asks anyway?

Don't be irritated. Show love. What I have learned is love is not always doing something for someone that they can't do for themselves. True love does things for a person they can do for themselves without hesitation or resentment. When we happily help our husbands with those things it speaks gentleness, helpfulness and humility.

Without any context clues, punctuation marks or other emphasis, I would like to know what tone you hear when I say the following statements:

Referring to my child: "He's a baby."

Referring to my husband: "He's a grown man."

I am confident in the first statement you heard a compassionate, sympathetic and helpful tone. In the second, however, the tone you associated with it was harsh, stern and unhelpful. We can safely draw these conclusions about the above statements without much information because of the common thought process of most women and wives. That thought process says "when my children need something it is because they can't. So I must. When my husband asks me to do something it is because he won't. So neither will I. If I do decide to do it, I won't be happy about it."

This thought process makes us view our husbands as selfish. We have told ourselves that anytime our husbands ask us to meet a need they can do on their own, they are taking advantage of us. We have to aggressively attack that negative train of thought.

*Survive Vs Thrive*

I estimate that 85% of our husbands' needs are things they can do for themselves. Think about it. Most of our husbands can cook well enough to survive, if not, they can easily go buy ready-made food. They can iron, if not, drop their clothes at the cleaners. They can clean a house or hire a maid. They can use a phone to schedule appointments, subtract well enough to balance a checkbook and do almost anything else independently.

If we are only nice about meeting the remaining 15% of our husbands' needs, the things they truly cannot do, then the majority of the time we will be acting in resentment believing that our husbands are selfish.

In Genesis, when God told Adam He was going to create for him a suitable helpmate, it was not out of necessity but companionship. Adam was independent. He named the animals on his own ability. Fed himself from the food in the garden without assistance. Adam held meetings with God without needing help articulating. He did not need Eve to survive. He needed her to thrive.

Our husbands can survive without us but how much they thrive can be largely dependent upon us. We have been put in their lives to add ease, comfort, organization and enjoyment.

In Genesis 2:18, God said he wanted to give Adam a "helper." When you think of the word help, do you have a vision of a servant? There is a book turned movie called *The Help.* The word help in the book refers to maids. When you read this verse in Genesis do you read it as "I will give you a maid suitable for you?" If this is how you view it, then this perception is causing you to be resentful of your role.

The Hebrew word used in Genesis 2 to describe Eve is "ezer." In her blog *New Life,* Marg Mowczko says that **ezer** is used only twenty-one times in the Old Testament. Twice it is used to refer to Eve. Three times the word is used in a military context. Sixteen times it is used in reference to God as a helper. All of these verses are using the word "helper" to describe a vital and powerful kind of help.

Further commentary from R. David Freedman breaks the word **ezer** down as a combination of two roots, meaning *"to rescue, to save," and "strength."*

Read a few verses where help is used elsewhere in scripture.

"I lift up my eyes to the mountains – where does my **help** come from? My **help** comes from the LORD, the Maker of heaven and earth" (Psalm 121:1-2).

"Our **help** is in the Name of the LORD, the Maker of heaven and earth" (Psalm 124:8).

"We wait in hope for the LORD; he is our **help** and shield" (Psalm 33:20).

For a complete list visit http://newlife.id.au/equality-and-gender-issues/a-suitable-helper/

Does using the biblical context of the word helper radically redefine your perception of your role? It should! Instead of thinking of yourself as a maid, think of yourself as a mighty force, a warrior and strength in the life of your husband.

Remember to be an ezer (help) in all situations, small or large, with grace and a smile.

*Open Doors Vs Cleaning Floors*

If we drilled it down, we would admit that children are cute leeches. They take our money, our energy and our time. In return, they take more of our money, energy and time. We know and accept as mothers we are the givers in that relationship.

As a wife though, we have an expectation of being the receiver. We know that there are things that we need to do for our husbands, but overall we expect to be taken care of, tended to and even pampered. We expect him to open a ton more car doors than we clean floors.

Entering marriage, I had no idea the degree of disproportion my expectations were. One specific example is how irritated I got when my husband called me from another room and asked me to come where he was. I got so angered that he expected me to stop what I was doing, leave the room I was in, and go to him. This may sound selfish or silly, but it was a small indicator light of unmet and disproportionate expectations. I realized that even in a small situation like this, I thought my husband should be the one to serve me, not the other way around. So now, as I strive to be a giver, when he says come, I go, and I still occasionally have to shake the urge to say, "No. You come to me."

As women, we dream about having someone wash the spot on our backs we can never reach on our own, someone to bring us flowers, go out on midnight pregnancy food runs, and take up for us when the guy in line is rude. We always dream about the moments when we are getting served. Not many of us dreamed or fanaticized about bringing him his plate, ironing his clothes, giving him a back rub or picking his underwear up from the floor.

As a single woman desiring marriage, I desired to be loved, not to fully love. There is a huge difference between the two. Wanting love receives the benefits from another. Fully loving gives with no requirement or expectation of reciprocity or obligation to repay.

It is not that we are intentionally or even knowingly wanting special treatment. We are wired to want it. That's another natural (fleshy) desire we have. It's ok to have it but it must be tamed. At the end of each day ask yourself, "how have I served my husband today and what has my attitude been towards it?"

It is always "more blessed to give than receive" (Acts 20:35). If you apply this in your relationship with your husband, your marriage and you as an individual, will begin to flourish.

Don't have the narrow mindset of only meeting your husband's needs. Be available to meet his "need of the moment." A need may be cooking dinner for the family. A need of the moment may be cutting up a whole pineapple for a snack when he randomly requests it. A need could be picking him up from work when the two of you are functioning on one car. A need of the moment could be driving to get his dry cleaning that he forgot on his way in from work.

*Mira Rollins*

*I Drew the Short Straw*

In many conversations with wives about marriage, many of us share a sense that we drew the short straw and that the men got the better deal. We can list in rapid fire style the adjustments we had to make to accommodate marriage and children, the increased responsibilities we have and the consistent emotional and physical catering we have to do for our husbands. It often feels as if they hit the lottery and we got an untrained, hyper and needy pet for Christmas.

When you hit the lottery (I wish I was telling you this from personal experience) your life options are open and endless. Your freedoms, opportunities, and responsibilities drastically improve. However, when you get a pet, though they bring you joy, they also come with lots of responsibilities. They require scooping poop, walks, bathing, veterinarian appointments, cleaning vomit when they eat something random outside (this one *is* from personal experience) and any number of laborious tasks.

Many wives feel as though their husbands' lives instantly and exponentially improved upon marriage. Yet they feel their own married life came with a mixed bag of joy and jobs—lots of them. This feeling creates resentment.

I admit I felt this way for the first eight and a half years of our marriage. My feelings towards marriage and my husband were daily influenced by this dark cloud of jealousy. I lived my life convinced that he owed me something because of what he gained and what I was unfairly burdened with.

Until one day I stopped to take inventory. Yes, I had one thousand and one daily responsibilities that were primarily mine. However, he had about 889 that were primarily his. (I am convinced I still have more than he does.) I stopped and tried to remember the last time I washed my own car, mowed the lawn, took out the trash, paid a light bill, picked my son up from a late night game, or waited for an oil change. When I got out of my emotions and really looked at the facts, my husband acquired lots of responsibility when he married me as well.

In most marriages, the distribution of responsibility is not as disproportionate as we tend to believe. Do your own inventory. Don't look for complete equality. Just take a general assessment and see if things nearly average out. I'm sure you will find you have been a little unfair to your man. It might turn out he is not that much of a leech after all.

There is no denying that marriage and motherhood are difficult jobs. Some days it is all you can do just to make it to the bed at the end of the day without crying or fainting first. However, your contribution to the world through your husband first and then your children, is of monumental importance. So a job of this magnitude should not be expected to always be easy. You are changing the world for the better, one perfectly starched shirt at a time.

Ponder:

What is something your husband asks you to do for him that has irritated you, because he can or should be able to do it for himself? How have you manifested your irritation to him regarding this situation?

Pray:

Grant me the humility and desire to show love to my husband by meeting his needs graciously, even those that he can do for himself.

Practice:

Do three things for your husband this week that he can fully do for himself without a negative attitude.

# FACEBOOK FUNNIES:

OK, so the police just left my house because my bad baby called 911 while playing on the phone. OMG. Time for bed.

— June 14, 2011

CHAPTER 5

# *The Mini Me's have it*

*The man said, "This is now bone of my bone and flesh of my flesh. She shall be called 'woman' for she was taken out of man."*
*Genesis 2:23*

Biting is a stage many toddlers go through. I know that. I read about it online. Talked to other moms about it. I even studied this as part of child development in college. Yet, when my son went through this stage, I convinced myself that I was solely responsible for his aggressiveness and solely responsible for fixing it.

This became my mission. When he had a day without biting, I was proud because my newest strategy had obviously worked. The next day, when I got the report from daycare that he bit again, I was distressed because obviously I had not done enough to put an end to this behavior. I took personal ownership and responsibility for my son's success and failure.

Whether grades in school, athletic performance or behavior, we take personal accountability for our children's behavior, the good and the bad. This "ownership" causes us to care more deeply, work smarter, reassess more and celebrate even louder.

However, with our husbands, oftentimes it's theirs, not ours. Whatever the "it" is, we label it as theirs. The highs, the lows, successes, failures, and all other transitions in our husbands are put on them to own. Yes, we help and give advice, but not at the same level of intensity that we partner with our children.

At the root of this issue is a lack of oneness with your spouse. The bible states in Matthew 9:5 "For this reason a man shall leave his father and mother and be joined to his wife, and the two shall become one."

Oneness is a hard concept to grasp. In a nutshell, oneness means the life, vision, responsibility, victories and losses of two people are equally shared. In everything. A healthy marriage cannot flourish in an environment where oneness is not present.

You may not be experiencing oneness in your relationship because...

- ❐ You are afraid of losing yourself. As women of the millennium, we have so much that is "ours." Our own jobs, friends, interests, hobbies, and money, just to name a few. With so much that is ours, it is a frightening thought to become one with someone else. We see it as moving into a small one-bedroom apartment. Everything from both houses just won't fit. So we are holding on for dear life to pieces of ourselves that are nonnegotiable. Willing to let go of a few, but prepared to fight for others. Ladies, oneness does not mean you lose your own identity and your personal interests. It means you take full interest in and responsibility of someone else's concerns and wellbeing and someone does the same for you. There will be compromises to be made, but in a healthy relationship, there is no threat of having to abandon "who you are."

- ❐ You are afraid to be vulnerable. In order to be one with someone else you have to fully let them in. You have to let them know your desires, your fears, and thoughts. If you do not let your husband "in" then oneness cannot be achieved. Here are two factors that could be preventing you from allowing your husband in:

- ☐ You have not had good female models who were comfortable with vulnerability. You have patterned yourself after emotionally defensive women.

- ☐ You fear that he will not like or respect the imperfect pieces of you, so you hide them from him. As women, we only let out what we like about ourselves.

- ☐ It's easier to cast blame than to accept it. If we don't take ownership of an issue, then we are never at fault. Many wives act selfishly by having a "this was *your* bright idea" attitude when things go wrong.

- ☐ You want the life of a single but the title of a wife. Are you struggling with "having to check in" when it's really just accountability? Or "feeling smothered" when it might be healthy quality time? Or "feeling financially micromanaged" when it's managing household finances?

All of the above scenarios boil down to using the world's wisdom inside of a Godly institution. It won't work! Abandon the old mindset. Resist those urges and patterns of thinking. Begin striving for oneness.

*How do two truly become one?*

With our children we feel a connectedness because they are from us. There is a literal sense of them being an extension of us. That sense of physical connectedness increases our care and compassion. Doing something for our children feels as if we are doing it for ourselves.

However, with our husbands we feel as if we are giving to another. We must pray the specific prayer that allows us to feel the oneness that God speaks of in Matthew 9:5.

We all have heard "leave and cleave" and "the two shall become one." If you are like me, you were confused on the actual process of making that happen. It sounds good but how is it accomplished?

Here are a few practical techniques that helped me.

*Share common goals and visions.* There was a cartoon called "Cat Dog". The main charter was a catdog. No I did not forget to put a space in catdog. The main character was an animal that was a cat at one end and a dog at the other. This was not one of my weekly television programs, promise. The few times that I caught bits and pieces of the show, I saw enough to see that Catdog operated in chaos. If Cat wanted to go right, Dog wanted to go left. If Dog wanted to sleep, Cat was ready to play. They were constantly pulling, forcing or dragging the other to move. Nothing was ever easy because they never shared the desire to move in the same direction. Though they were connected, they were not actually one.

How about you and your spouse? Do you want to go in the same direction as your husband? What is your shared financial vision for your family? What spiritual vision do you both support? Do you like to watch any of the same television shows? Is there shared vision for your family or do you each have to constantly drag the other person to save or invest? If most conversations are spent debating, convincing or arguing, then you are most likely connected by the marriage vows but not experiencing oneness.

Make a commitment to sit down with your husband and have a meeting about your short-term goals and long-term visions. Get aligned. Get on the same page. This will be the first step to experiencing oneness.

*By being honest and intimate.* Once on a popular daytime talk show, there was a couple who had been married for over 10 years, shared at least two children, yet the wife would not allow her husband to see her brush her teeth. He had seen her ill, give birth and in several other very personal situations, but for some reason, the thought of her husband seeing her brush her teeth was unbearable. If he tried to come in while she was brushing her teeth she would force him out of the bathroom, shut and lock the door.

*Acing Motherhood But Failing Marriage*

The studio audience was in shock, as I was, that this woman was not comfortable with her husband. This likely sounds unreasonable to you as well, but are there areas of your life that you are not comfortable allowing your husband to see? Where have you pushed your husband away? Where have you shut your husband out? What areas of your heart have you locked your husband out? In order to become one with him, you must let him in, all the way.

Over anyone else and even if no one else, your husband should know you. The good, the bad, and the ugly.

*By allowing your husband to be honest and intimate.* With my son I did not experience the terrible twos. Wait before you tell me how lucky I am because he went through the tumultuous threes. At this stage, he was either repeating something inappropriate, climbing on something potentially deadly, or leaving tornado-like destruction everywhere he went.

During this season, one of his difficult behaviors centered around his utter refusal to wear clothes when home. Many visitors were greeted by my son running around the house naked. I thought about changing his name to Adam, because he was truly "naked and unashamed." I tried everything to break this habit. Many months passed and he was still a three foot streaker. In one instance in sheer frustration, I raised my voice as I saw him descending the stairs naked and yelled in frustration, "Go put on some clothes!"

He looked at me in complete confusion and bewilderment and asked, "Why?"

His response was not out of disrespect or ignorance but something much deeper. In one word he conveyed a deep truth about our relationship. What his mind was thinking, his three-year-old vocabulary could not articulate. What he wanted to say was this: "Mom, I'm at home. It's just you and me. What's the big deal? I am completely comfortable with you seeing me completely exposed."

Is your husband completely comfortable with being completely exposed in your presence? Have you created a safe and nonjudgmental environment in which he can tell you his secrets, his faults, and his dreams? Can he share his fears with you, knowing you will never discuss them with your best friend or mother? Can he honestly confide his temptations and struggles without fear of accusations and judgment? Can your husband share his needs without fear of being labeled as unappreciative and selfish? Are you able to do the same?

When you and your husband are together, does it feel like Eden? A place of complete nakedness yet complete comfort. A place where both of you feel protected, encouraged and accepted.

*By intertwining your daily lives.* In our early twenties, my sister and I lived together. We shared a bedroom all of our childhood. We both vowed once we moved out of our childhood home, that would be the last time we cohabitated. I was the typical bratty younger sister. She was the typical bossy and "too cool to be bothered" older sister. Years later, we both had either forgotten how horrible the experience was or matured enough to figure it would be different.

It actually worked out great. I can't say it was because of my newfound maturity. It was simply because we rarely saw each other. We had completely different schedules. We were like two ships in the night, passing and interacting for only brief moments. We shared living quarters but we did not share a life.

This arrangement worked perfectly for my sister and me but cannot work for a thriving marriage. In order to become one, the two of you have to mix your lives together. I am not suggesting that you have no life outside of him: no people, places or pastimes of your own. I am saying; however, that if you have different friends, different bank accounts, different hobbies, different workout schedules, different sleep schedules, different *everything,* then it will be impossible for the two of you to become one.

Stop being afraid to let go of "who you are." Holding on so tightly to *you* is making you lose *him*. If you won't let go of you, there will never be a true *"y'all."* (I just let a little Texas slip out on that last word.)

*Compliment, don't compete.*

Another stage my middle son went through is one of constant competition. In everything he had to be first. First to finish his food. First to buckle his seat belt. First to get out of the car and into the house, to turn on the TV, and to get dressed.

One night when I announced it was time for bed, he zipped past my daughter and me, and ran up the stairs to his bedroom. Once he made it there, he turned around and proclaimed his victory, "First!"

My daughter was several steps behind him and once she arrived she yelled with just as much excitement and as much enthusiasm, "Second!" Either she did not know, or did not care that she was "competing."

She was not in it, to win it. She just wanted to enjoy the experience.

Do you function in your marriage like my son (always competing) or my daughter (enjoying the experience)?

Unfortunately, I believe that many women feel the need to be in constant competition.

- ❒ Competing to be your boss's right-hand woman for fear of being replaced by the new hire.
- ❒ Competing to be your parents' favorite out of concern that they will be disappointed with you.
- ❒ Competing to be the best in your workout class to show the younger women that you still "got it."

This also spills over into your marriage.

You want to be the kids' favorite so they think you are the fun parent. You want to show your husband your job is just as important as his. You stress yourself out cleaning the house to show your husband you are just as good at cleaning as his mother. You are on a crazy diet and workout regimen to be as fit as your husband's ex-girlfriend.

If we are not careful, we will miss out on the enjoyment of the experience of marriage. More importantly, competition cancels out oneness. Our need to compete could be destroying our relationships with our husbands.

*Marriage is not a competition but there is a prize to be One*

We must desire to form a mentality that says we are on the same team. When there is a disagreement, don't focus on winning but on what decision will truly work best for your household. This does not mean we have to agree on everything. It does mean that we have to play on the same side in everything.

In a football game, when a coach calls a play that a particular player does not like, that player may voice his opinion as to why he does not think that's the best idea. Hopefully, his opposition to the play has nothing to do with how it will affect him *individually* but the *team* collectively. In your disagreements with your spouse, has the majority of your opposition been due to how it affects you or the household?

After the coach hears the player's reasoning on why the player disagrees with the play, many times the coach will still go with his initial call. Other times the coach will not even entertain the player's disagreement because either of time sensitivity or his certainty of his decision. That player gets on the field and executes the play with 100% effort, as if it were his own. Why? He understands oneness. He doesn't see it as losing an argument. He sees it simply as the coach thinking another play would be best for the team.

The player is able to execute in this manner because he

- ☐ has a healthy level of trust in his coach's abilities
- ☐ has a mature respect for the coach's position
- ☐ has a desire to advance the team over himself
- ☐ has the ability to distinguish "play calling" from being "picked on."

Which of these four do you struggle with?

Many times in the middle of a disagreement when my husband and I find ourselves in a bad game of tug of war, one of us reminds the other "Same team, remember? Same team." Are you on your husband's team?

Take a moment to answer the following questions:

1. Where in my marriage am I unnecessarily competing?

2. What emotion is driving me to compete (insecurity, fear, pride, etc.)?

3. How is my need to compete negatively impacting my relationship?

4. How does competition change the atmosphere of my home?

5. What are specific things I can do to stop competing with my husband?

Ladies, life is not a competition. It's an experience. Stop racing and just start living.

Ponder:

What secrets are you holding from your husband? What haven't you shared with your husband out of fear of judgment?

Pray:

God, please give me the strength to be vulnerable.

Practice:

Now armed with the strength of vulnerability, share something with your husband he does not know about you.

# FACEBOOK FUNNIES:

Eric Rollins happy birthday boyfriend! Friend! Work out partner! Dress zipper when my arms won't reach! Car washer! Daddy! Bread winner! Travel buddy! Griller! Chick flick movie partner! And basically the guy I picked to do the rest of my life with.

— July 20, 2015

CHAPTER 6

## *He's not the same man I married*

*And Jesus kept increasing in wisdom and stature, and in favor with God and men. Luke 2:52*

I remember holding my youngest as she snuggled under my arm as an infant. She didn't cry much and was a calm baby and easy to soothe. Then something happened. She became a screaming terror. Her appetite intensified. She aggressively made it known she was hungry. Then she began teething, so her attitude got real ugly. As she grew to a toddler, things calmed down a little. She was learning to walk and she wanted to explore. My once calm child that just wanted to snuggle became an energetic toddler on the move.

With each stage, I related to her differently. I understood that at two years old, she was not the same person she was at two months old. She had different experiences. She was literally seeing life from a different vantage point. As she moved in and out of stages, I adjusted how I related to her.

Children are not the only people moving through stages. Adults are as well. Our husbands move through stages. Their life experiences change them. Deaths, births, lay-offs, promotions, sicknesses, education, children and all other live experiences push him into different life stages. In each stage, your husband will be different. In one stage he may be more jovial and in another more serious. In one certain stage he may be clingy but in another he may desire more time alone.

If we are unable to adjust to our husbands as they move through life stages, it will be harmful to him and the marriage. His patterns, preferences and personality have changed, so you can't use the same methods to relate to him. The man you married on your wedding day is not the same man he is now. Some of you are saying "Praise the good Lord" while others of you are saying "I miss that guy." In either case, it requires awareness and flexibility from you to bring out the best in your husband in each changing stage of his life.

Your understanding of this is critical. Often times, there will not be a significant warning sign to alert you that your husband is moving into a different stage. No blinking billboard with an arrow over his head will appear. The window of time to make a smooth transition with your husband will most often be narrow. This is why we must stay tuned in and connected to our spouses.

Make it a point to study your husband, his moods, habits and personality. When you have taken the time to study him, you will quickly pick up the subtle signs that his life stage is changing. Also, do frequent "check-ins." On a regular basis, ask him direct questions about how he is doing. Warning ladies, don't just ask "How are you doing?" "Fine" will not be enough to get you the info you need. Ask him questions that require responses of more than one word. Here is a list of 10 questions that are great for routine check-ins:

1. Do you feel you are getting enough time to do the things you enjoy? If not, I am open to scheduling some consistent time every week for you to get a break.

2. Do you feel you are getting enough rest? Is there anything in our schedule that you want to look at adjusting in order to give you a little more time to recuperate?

3. Do you have any suggestions or concerns regarding the kids' schedules or behavior?

4. What is your assessment of our financial decisions and progress this month?

5. Is there anything at work that is causing you stress?

6. What has made you happy this week?

7. Name one thing you would like to change about your life.

8. Name one thing you would like to celebrate.

9. What's keeping you up at night?

10. On a scale of 1 – 10, 1 being awful and 10 being awesome, how would you rank your life right now?

Each of the above questions can be the catalyst for great discussion to get a sense of how your husband is really doing. He needs you to do a "gut check" periodically to see where he is emotionally in various areas of his life. Whether you use any, all or none of the above questions, make sure you use some method to intentionally check in with your spouse.

Though "check ins" will reduce the chance of your husband morphing from Dr. Jekyll to Mr. Hyde without any prior warning, some changes will occur suddenly. Normally these drastic changes are caused by sudden life events such as deaths, unplanned layoffs, or health issues. During these times, be full of grace, humility and strategy.

There will also be times when he is different and you have absolutely no idea why. At these times you will have to adjust without fully understanding "What's the deal with him?" When you don't fully understand what caused him to move into a different stage, still make the proper adjustments. Continue to seek what caused him to move into this stage, but don't wait on the understanding before you adjust. Action is required before understanding.

*Awareness*

If you don't realize that your husband has moved into a different stage, then you will relate to him the same. Doing so can cause miscommunication, tension, and division between you.

Consider this example. Normally you and your husband are inseparable. The two of you worked out together, went to dinner and movies together, vacationed together and did everything as a couple. Lately, he has been going to a different room to watch television. He also has been going for morning runs alone instead of going to the gym with you. You've also noticed that he has been making plans to golf with a friend more often than usual.

You are convinced he doesn't like spending time with you anymore. You are racking your brain attempting to figure out if you are boring him, offended him or completely losing him. You feel too embarrassed to ask. So for weeks, you have suffered in silence, wondering if your husband is slipping away.

When in actuality, he's just in a different stage. With his recent lay off, he's been feeling a little insecure. It helps to talk some of these insecurities out with his male friends. He also has been more stressed about household finances and finding employment. Running helps him work off some steam. You don't run. Actually the only time you run is if something is chasing you. So he doesn't ask you to go with him because he knows your hatred for running.

What you perceived as isolation and distance, is just your husband moving in a different life stage. It has nothing to do with you. He is not seeing someone else. He is not ready for a divorce. So just adjust with him.

You will have to study your husband because men are not typically talkers. Like our toddlers, men have trouble "using their words."

Women use about 20,000 words per day while men use an average of 7000. It is clear that men speak mostly out of necessity.

It is not that men are not intelligent or inarticulate. They are just uncomfortable with emotional conversations. Knowing this, we must sometimes rely on observation instead of conversation when assessing our spouses' needs.

*Acing Motherhood But Failing Marriage*

*Name the Stage*

Realize that saying your husband is in a good stage or bad stage is not specific enough. You should take the time to assess your husband and study him to see if he is in a stage of denial, a stage of loss, a stage of insecurity or fear. Once you correctly identify what stage or stages your husband is in, it will help you interact with him appropriately.

Most research conducted these days recognizes different stages of life. These stages, however, are driven by age. Claudius Ptolemy was the first to develop this concept back in ancient Greece. He defined the stages as infant, childhood, teenager, young adult, adulthood, retirement and finally, elderly.

Then there is another popular model regarding the stages of grief. Denial and isolation, anger, bargaining, depression and then acceptance.

I believe there are still 100 more stages that adults experience based on any number of life issues. There is a stage of "I'm tired of runny-nosed kids and noise." If your husband is going through this stage, don't think he is a horrible father and you will have to raise your kids alone. No, he is just overwhelmed by the reality of his life as a father. He is having to accept that his days of spontaneous nights out with his wife are over. That spending Sundays all day in his man cave watching football are over. It might be a little too much for him right now, so he may detach a little just to get his second wind. Allow him this time. He will make a strong comeback.

How about the "I don't want to help clean up" stage. This does not mean he doesn't love you or that he is taking you for granted or that he will forever be a slob. This might just mean that he is really tired from long days at work and when he gets home, all he wants to do is lounge. This too will pass. When things calm down at work and when he gets a little more evening energy, he will again help out as he used to.

Your interaction and support of your husband during each stage plays a huge role in how quickly he moves out of it or how long he stays in it. If it is a "bad" stage then the sooner you give him the support he needs, the quicker he will be able to move from it. And if it is a "good" stage, the more you positively reinforce him, the longer the stage will last.

*Leaves and Roots*

When we understand our husbands move through different life stages, we will change our view of them. We will give them the same consideration for growth that we do our children.

The last time a friend or family member asked how your son was doing you said "Girl, pray for him. He is just doing a lot of selfish things these days." But when they ask that same question about your husband your response is "Girl, pray for me; he is the most selfish man I have ever met." See the difference?

We are careful not to label our children but take great ease in doing so with our husbands. Have you ever been in a room when someone called a little child the "B" word, Bad? The entire room gasps and people everywhere chime in to correct. "There are no bad children, just good children with bad behavior." Another angered parent piggybacks on the comment and says "No bad children, just bad choices."

As wives, we must be as diligent not to label our husbands as "bad." Recognize the stage that is driving the "bad behavior." View the behavior as a leaf that needs to be shed, not as a rotten root. Your husband is not a bad man with bad behavior. He is a good man with imperfections. The ability to separate imperfections from the person is critical in the survival of relationships.

Ponder:

If you had to label the current stage your husband, what would it be?

Pray:

God, please give me the wisdom and patience to properly interact with my husband during this stage of his life.

Practice:

Identify and do or say three specific things for your husband that will be beneficial to him during his current life stage.

## FACEBOOK FUNNIES:

OK, if you are one of the people who know my husband, then you know if I let today go by without giving him a shout out, then I will have some trouble to pay. So to Eric Rollins, thank you for being a wonderful father. I make fun of you when you are brought to tears by watching one of our 3 kids take their first steps, or play their first baseball game or make a touchdown. It's amazing. You bring the fun to their lives. I look forward to seeing the adults they become because of the father you are.

— Father's Day 2015

CHAPTER 7

# Amnesia Vs Post Traumatic Stress Disorder (PTSD)

*"I, even I, am he who blots out your transgressions, for my own sake and remembers your sins no more" Isaiah 43:25.*

Has your son ever thrown a level 10 temper tantrum that not only left you extremely embarrassed in public but also made you late to an important meeting? Has your daughter missed curfew after promising to be respectful of the time you agreed to and left you worrying about her safety because she was too absentminded to call? Have your children caused you stress, embarrassment, money, unnecessary energy, grief or a combination of these. Think about the worst thing your child has ever done. How long did it take you to "get over it" and forgive him or her? If you are like me, when incidents first occur you threaten a punishment fit for a death row inmate. However, with a little good behavior on their part we completely pardon them.

When our children offend, disobey or disappoint us we handle it like a traumatic event followed by amnesia. We are upset, cry, yell and get angry. When the dust settles though, we hold no grudges and restore them back to full fellowship. Oftentimes, once their behavior is back in line, we forget all about the previous offense. They once again become our little angels.

When our husbands' offend, disagree with, or disappoint us, we handle it like post-traumatic stress disorder. We say we forgive, but it takes one trigger, one misspoken word, or one mistake and we are back at the same place we were when the incident first occurred. The negative emotions come forcefully rushing back as if they never left.

Because they didn't!

We forgive our children but we furlough our husbands. One definition of a furlough is a temporary leave of absence authorized for a prisoner from a penitentiary. When our husbands offend us, we sentence them to a period of anger, distrust, and distance. Then at some point, we begin to have a better relationship with them again, seemingly acting in forgiveness. But when that trigger hits, we place them back in a jail cell of attitude, anger and resentment all over again. Now he realizes he was never really forgiven, just furloughed.

We have to truly learn to forgive our husbands. Many of us genuinely desire true forgiveness but actually don't know what it is, much less how to actually do it. If we are honest, forgiveness is one of those concepts in scripture that we believe only the holiest of holiest can achieve.

*What is Forgiveness*

The first step in forgiveness is truly understanding what it is and what it is not. Here are a few definitions to bring clarity to this seemingly unattainable and lofty concept.

1. To excuse for a fault or an offense; pardon.

2. To renounce anger or resentment against.

3. To absolve from payment of (a debt, for example).

(The Free dictionary by Farlex)

Even with such concise and precise definitions, I am thinking a little personalization may be helpful to do a better gut check.

Think of an issue you have told your spouse and yourself that you have forgiven him for. Enter that situation in the blanks below and assess if after reading each statement, you can attest to the truth of that statement.

- ☐ Regarding the incident in which you _____, I have released you from any and all negative consequences of that offense. I have shown evidence of this through my consistent interaction with you.

- ☐ Regarding the incident in which you _____, I do not think of or interact with you in a way that demonstrates any anger or resentment. I have shown evidence of this through my pure, genuine and encouraging thoughts and behaviors.

- ☐ Regarding the incident in which you _____, you do not owe me anything. No further words or actions are required from you to restore our full fellowship. I have shown evidence of this through my consistent, positive interaction with you.

After analyzing these statements, have you furloughed or forgiven?

*How do I forgive?*

Most of us know the textbook definitions of forgiveness. Few of us know what that looks like in reality.

Here are a few examples of how to carry out the task of forgiveness:

- ☐ Give up the right to hear I'm sorry. – I began with this one because this is the most difficult for me. My struggle is what I feel to be Forgiveness 101: If you don't ask for forgiveness then you don't get it. To me, it is just that simple. However, it is not up to me. Jesus modeled otherwise. While on the cross, he asked the Father to forgive those who were crucifying Him, without their recognition of their wrong. Following this model, we must forgive people even in situations when they have yet to (or never) acknowledged the offense against us. Forgiveness is easiest when it is a request granted but it is deepest when it is an unsolicited gift.

◻ Let go of the negative emotion of an issue while someone is still offending you. Using the model of the cross again, Jesus asked the Father to forgive those that were violently taking his wife *while* they were crucifying him. We must also follow this example. This is not the same as allowing someone to continue to offend you. However, it does mean that you grant forgiveness even if the person has not yet changed their behavior. You set boundaries to protect yourself from the offense but you also set boundaries against bitterness taking root in your heart.

◻ Don't allow the offense to affect how you treat them. True forgiveness has visible and verifiable proof of how you relate to someone. How are your tone and your temper? Is the interaction cold and callused or warm and welcoming?

◻ Wish good for and not ill towards that person. Wanting the person to be punished is a sign that you have not forgiven yet. Forgiveness asks for a pardon for someone on their behalf.

◻ Have a long fuse and not one that is always ready to go off. If you are always near the emotional edge with someone who has previously offended you, then you are still operating in un-forgiveness. Patience, compassion and helpfulness are signs of forgiveness.

What forgiveness is not...

◻ Continuing to allow someone to mistreat you by being naïve, vulnerable or in denial

◻ Ignoring an issue

◻ Avoiding confronting the situation with the person

◻ Not using appropriate consequences for another's bad behavior

◻ Being passive and not addressing negative behaviors aimed towards you

Reasons we are fearful or hesitant to forgive…

- ☐ If I forgive him, then what will be the negative consequence that will deter him from doing it again.
- ☐ If I forgive him, how will he know how deeply he offended me?
- ☐ If I forgive him, then he will think I am weak.
- ☐ If I forgive him, others will think I am weak.
- ☐ I don't want to forgive him.

*Benefits of forgiveness*

- ☐ Matthew 6:14-15 "For if you forgive others their trespasses, your heavenly Father will also forgive you, but if you do not forgive others their trespasses, neither will your Father forgive your trespasses."
- ☐ Proverbs 12:16 "The vexation of a fool is known at once, but the prudent ignores an insult."
- ☐ Mark 11:25 "But when you are praying, first forgive anyone you are holding a grudge against, so that your Father in heaven will forgive your sins, too."

I have learned that most successful marriages are those that can forgive much and forgive often. It is necessary to forgive daily. Life is most often lived in the middle not in the extremes. Meaning that yes, marriages will face situations such as adultery or severe financial mismanagement. But most often the issues that couples face are a harsh tone taken, forgetting an important event or not offering enough help at home. So forgiveness of the "little things" is important to the life of a marriage. Proverbs 19:11 encourages us all to "overlook many offenses." So what others may call naïve, the bible calls wise.

One technique to use to get over the little things quicker is to always assume positive intent. When your husband makes a comment that feels insulting, give him the benefit of the doubt by saying "I don't think that is how he meant to say that." Or when he does something that irritates you to no end, give him a pass by saying "I don't believe he tried to make me mad on purpose."

As wives, we are responsible for the atmosphere of our home. We must consistently forgive or else we will walk around each day with a negative attitude that will infest our homes much like carbon monoxide. Slowly, silently, but surely strangling the life out of our spouses, children, ourselves and our marriages.

However, if we learn to truly forgive, our attitude will change immediately. You will not always feel on edge. You won't be snappy with your husband or children. You won't feel used or mistreated. You will be able to interact with your husband, even in the presence of his errors, with "a peace that surpasses all understanding that will guard your hearts and your minds in Christ Jesus" (Philippians 4:7). The spirit of forgiveness will be so strong that it will be nearly tangible. Almost visible. It will manifest in a spirit of calm and peace that will radically change the entire atmosphere of your home. Forgiveness is a supernatural empowerment from God that results in supernatural gifts from God.

Ponder:

What are the issues that keep you angry with your husband? List them all. Don't think, just write. Number them as you go. After compiling this list, say this aloud, "I will forgive him for number 1 (fill in the blank). Then say I will forgive him for number 2 (fill in the blank). Go through the entire list, saying them aloud. Then recite Psalms 103:12 "as far as the east is from the west, so far has He removed our transgressions from us." In the shadow of understanding God's forgiveness of you, now it is time to do the same for your husband. Ball the paper up, go to the trashcan and throw it away.

Pray:

Teach me how to forgive. Increase my desire to forgive. Increase my awareness of how you daily forgive me so I can extend that forgiveness to my husband.

Practice:

Forgiveness. When you feel the urge to give him the silent treatment, go strike up a pleasant conversation. When he wants to go to the gym with you after an argument, agree to go instead of staying home and sulking. It will feel like he is winning, but it is actually you forgiving.

# FACEBOOK FUNNIES:

Shouting out to my wonderful husband who has been home with 7 kids for two days straight. He is an awesome dad. Thanks baby, you are a great dad and uncle.

— Dec 19, 2011

CHAPTER 8

## *Who's the Boss?*

*Therefore, humble yourselves under the mighty hand of God, that He may exalt you at the proper time. 1 Peter 5:6*

My oldest son is 16 years old and at the stage of always wanting to be away from home or having a friend over. Most weekends I either feel like I only have 2 children because my oldest is never there or I have 5 children because his friends are always over. His father, two siblings and I have officially been deemed as boring and uncool.

As with most teens, he views Saturdays as total fun days. One particular Saturday he wanted to go to the birthday party of one of his friends. However, he had not done several of his weekly chores. He had not cleaned his room, his bathroom, or vacuumed downstairs. I informed him that his responsibilities at the house come before activities outside of the house. He came up with a plan of cleaning the house that seemed reasonable to him but not to me. So after about 5 minutes of patiently allowing him to state his case, I still said no. Making it clear at this point that it was a non-negotiable no. He was visibly upset, but I knew I was correct in holding him to his responsibilities.

Now let's consider a similar incident. I told my husband I wanted to attend an upcoming Saturday morning conference. As with most families, Saturdays for us can be extremely busy. He reminded me that he needed my help at our yogurt shop that morning. I suggested that he handle the yogurt shop duties on his own this one time. He said although that would be possible, it would be very difficult because there were a few larger projects needing our attention in addition to our normal Saturday routine. I still thought that he could handle these despite the slight inconvenience. He then added that our normal childcare options would not be available and that he would have to take both of our smaller children to work with him. I figured out a timeline of child exchange between the two of us that sounded reasonable to me. He didn't like the plan at all. So after about 10 minutes of negotiations, he said that he did not think it was a good idea for me to go and that he needed me to go with him. In other words, a non-negotiable no. I was visibly, verbally and plain ol' mad.

I am a grown woman and it does not sit well with me to be told no. But as I compare the two situations, they are very similar, practically the same scenario. A person in a role of authority makes a fair decision based on the greater needs of the group that goes against the wishes of one. When I describe the scene without using names it sounds very rational. When I describe the scene inserting my son's name as the subordinate and my name as the person in authority it sounds logical. But when I replay the scene with me as the subordinate, it feels wrong, all wrong.

It is easy for us to give rules, expectations and standards to our children but very difficult for us to receive them from our husbands. We have told ourselves our issue with submission is due to our husbands' inability to effectively lead us or his unfairness. But as in my example above, many times our husbands' decisions are fair, we just don't like them. If the main issue is not that our husbands are leading irresponsibly, then what is it? I believe we find our answer in the first example of a woman not submitting to her husband, Eve.

After eating the fruit herself and offering it to Adam, God punishes Satan, Adam and Eve. We often discuss labor pains as Eve's punishment but rarely do we dive into the second part of her consequence. Exodus 3:16 says "the desire will be for your husband but he will rule over you." Here, desire does not mean an emotional or sexual desire of wanting your husband. It means that we will have a desire to dominate our husbands. A consequence of Eve's sin passed to all wives is the frustration and struggle of attempting to rule over our spouses.

The reason it is extremely difficult to submit to our husbands is because we have an evil fleshly desire to rule over him passed on to us by Eve. (Another reason I am hunting her down when I get to heaven.)

We must not submit to that urge, but fight against it. The next time your husband "rules" in a situation and that familiar feeling of anger swells within you, pray it away. Know that it is most likely your "Eve complex" talking.

*Submission has gotten a bad rap*

Even though we now realize that the urge to dominate our husbands is real and passed on by Eve, it still does not make the task of submission any easier to carry out. Remember, we behave as we believe. Here's a table that will hopefully help you change your view of submission.

| Is Not… | Is… |
| --- | --- |
| Going passively along with any and every thing suggested by your husband | Allowing your husband space, grace and permission to lead by implementing new goals, ideas and visions |
| Never providing feedback or suggestions | Allowing your husband time and space to figure things out without jumping to do it your way and in your timing |
| Being forced into the shadows of silence | Being slow to speak. Reserving and taming your opinion as needed for the situation. |
| Standing by idly and helplessly watching your household fall and your husband lead the family to destruction | Allowing your husband time for trial and error in appropriate situations |
| Tolerating consistent negative criticism, being ridiculed and torn down | Giving your husband permission and being receptive to critical feedback. |

The world would have us believe that submission is everything in the "Is Not" category. The world lies. It is up to us not to buy the lie.

*Position not Price*

Submission is not about our value or worth, it's about function and order. I am just as valuable to God, to my household and to the world as my husband. However, I voluntarily yield to him to allow the smooth functioning of my household. Submission happens everywhere. We don't mind it in other areas, so we should not fight against it at home. See the examples of submission below:

- Five equally talented basketball players on a court. Only one calls the plays.
- Two brand new luxury cars on the road. One exiting the freeway and the other on the service road. One allows the other to go first.
- An army squad of equally trained fighters. Only one captain. The others wait on his command before attacking.

In each of the above examples, we understand why submission is necessary. It allows for order, effectiveness, progress and desired results. Without submission there is no success. If you want a successful marriage, with successful kids, with success in business and finance, you must submit.

Thinking of this made me evaluate myself in situations where I have the opportunity to "submit" by showing grace, love, kindness or forgiveness, at the risk of being perceived as weak. For example, when someone is riding my bumper in traffic because they want me to either go faster or move, do I move to a different lane and allow them to pass or do I slow down and box them in between me and the car next to us?

When in group meetings or discussions where I am the more experienced or knowledgeable participant, do I rush to give opinions and answers, or do I allow others the opportunity to share?

When someone is being rude, do I make it a point to be ruder, louder, and more hurtful? Or do I stay calm and even apologize for anything that I could have done to make them respond to me that way?

During my self-evaluation, I realized that I often choose to take the position of power and not humility. Of wanting to present myself as knowledgeable more than nice. Or superior rather than supportive.

So today, my challenge to you and to me, is to model ourselves after Christ. In Philippians 2:5-6 Jesus encourages us to "have this attitude in yourselves which was also in Christ Jesus who although He existed in the form of God, did not regard equality with God a thing to be grasped, but emptied himself, taking the form of a bond servant, and being made in the likeness of men, and being found in appearance as a man, He humbled Himself by becoming obedient to the point of death, even death on a cross."

Simply put, Jesus was fully God. Not some watered down, less powerful rookie. He was 100% God but respected his position. He chose the road of humility in order to advance the shared goal and vision. How about you?

*Action Before or Without Understanding*

Children have a tendency to want to know "why?" Eat your carrots. Why? Don't play in the water. Why? Time for bed. Why?

Most parents are irritated and upset by children's need to have clarification before they comply. It is viewed as disrespect. How many times have you said "Because I said so!" or "Just do it!"

As wives, we have to agree to follow our husbands without always knowing full details. I am not suggesting we have blind allegiance to everything he says. I am not suggesting that you become a puppet and not a partner. However, I am encouraging you to use wisdom and humility to know when you need to "just do it." This will demonstrate to your husband the level of trust and respect you have for him and his leadership.

People often discuss a woman's or a mother's intuition but rarely highlight a man's instinctive nature. God has given men discernment in areas that we have not been blessed with. Much of it centers around their ability to think less emotionally and more factually. They are able to see things that our emotions impede us from seeing.

Recently our eldest son came home after curfew and had an outlandish and nearly unbelievable series of events that caused it. As he gave such specific details I began to believe the unbelievable. My husband was not swayed at all. As my husband drilled him, my son became increasingly upset that his dad thought there was more to the story. Then I became upset because I felt bad for my son. I became wrapped up in the emotion of "what if he is telling the truth."

Well 24 hours and several investigative calls later, the full story unfolded. When the last detail dropped, my husband turned to me and said "I knew there was more. I know this is going to sound weird, but I could smell fear coming from him."

I laughed and waited on him to laugh as well, thinking he was exaggerating and being figurative. He then looked at me with a very stern and serious look and assured me, he literally sensed as our son walked in the door that there was something to this situation that we needed to dig to find out.

We must allow our husbands to use their senses to lead. Even if they can't or just don't provide you all the details, just follow. Don't always seek complete clarification before you comply. Don't mandate agreement before action. Information is not a prerequisite of submission.

*Submission = Selfishness*

I wanted ice cream. He said we did not have time to stop. Why is he so selfish?

I wanted to spend Christmas with my extended family. He decided to do Christmas with just the five of us. How could he be so uncaring?

I really felt I needed a few new outfits for work. He relayed to me that was not in the budget for this month. How could he be such a dictator?

Looking back, I have cried a river of tears over the "inconsiderate, uncaring, selfish oppressor" I married. When actually, it was simply a man being a leader. Many times a man will have to make a decision that is not your preference. Do not put a negative label on him because he is operating in his role.

It will take maturity on your part to disagree with a decision your husband makes without pouting, casting insults or harboring resentment. Though being a leader often appears to be the most desirable position, it is a difficult and stressful job. Most of our husbands want to please us but often have to make decisions that don't. They might not let on, but that is an intimidating and taxing responsibility. Allow him the ability to operate in his role without fear of the backlash.

*How can I submit when he is ruling unfairly?*

In speaking with many women, there is a shared complaint of a "double standard" at work in their homes. A general belief that the husband wants things from his wife that he does not consistently give. For example, he gets the urge to go watch a football game with friends. This happens when the mood strikes him. This has not been mentioned or previously discussed. He feels that because you two are not "doing anything" or don't have any plans, then he feels it's ok. So he leaves you with the kids for several hours while he goes out with his friends. This would be okay, except for your perception that the same liberty is not given you. You remember a specific example just last week that you wanted to catch a movie with your sister, but you didn't go because your husband said that he wasn't prepared to watch the children and he just needed to get some rest and it was too "spur of the moment."

Not fair, right? How many times have you said that word recently? Does the feeling of unfairness and inequality anger you?

Take a second and reflect on Philippians 2: 5-6. Remember, Jesus "did not regard equality with God something to be grasped." Are you fighting for complete equity in your marriage? It sounds logical. But it's not biblical.

Hard to swallow and I don't like it either, but as the popular saying goes, "It is what it is." Like Jesus, we should not regard equality with the person we have chosen to submit to as something to be grasped.

Need examples? Here are some of my own. When my kids were infants and started to cry, and Eric and I were both sitting on the couch relaxing, I tended to them a ratio of 8 to 2. A sink full of dishes would have *my* name metaphorically written on them, not his. He would have more ease getting away for alone time than I would. But the harder I fought for equality, the more I missed the point. The point is that there will be "inequalities" based on my function. Yes we both clean, but I serve as the primary homemaker. So on Saturday mornings if he "finishes" his cleaning and I still have floors to mop and clothes left to fold, it's ok. If we are both sitting comfortably on the couch and my then two-year-old walked past leaving a horrible scent in her wake, then that task had my name on it. Not quite fair, but it's just how it is.

There are "inequalities" that benefit me as well. For example, if there is any deficit in our household finances it is up to him to figure out how to close that gap. We both work, yes, but my function is not primary bread winner. If my children begin to have behavior issues, it is up to him to figure out the solution. Yes, we both discipline our children but his function is primary disciplinarian. If we both oversleep and are awakened by the sound of the trash truck, it is his responsibility to jump from bed partially dressed to get the bags to the curb in time. In these situations, I never raise the question of fairness or disparity.

Ladies, whether you like the truth of it or not, inequalities in your marriage will exist and you should not expect or even desire all things equal.

*Will You or Won't You*

A previous counselor of mine once told me that obedience is a decision of the will. As it relates to submission, at some point you just have to take that leap and obey. (Big Gulp. Still hard for me to swallow as well.)

Will you submit to your husband even when he…

Is wrong?

Is too slow to complete something?

Is too fast in doing something?

Is untactful about it?

Is arrogant in the way he completes it?

Will you submit to your husband even when you know you are…

Right?

Faster doing it?

More thorough?

More tactful?

Better at it?

Please be clear, the only time it is right to refuse to submit to your husband is when it is a matter of sin or safety. If what your husband is calling you to do is in opposition to what God calls you to do (sin), then you have the right and responsibility to follow God and not your husband. If there is a situation that puts you or your children in physical danger, then here too, you have the right and responsibility not to submit to your husband.

Most times, submission is not about sin or safety, but pride and preferences. Many times submitting to your husband will be costly and there may be negative results from submitting, but the long term benefits will be well worth it. Even if those benefits are not immediately seen, please do not grow weary in your well doing because in due season, you will reap your reward. (Galatians 6:9)

Even if submitting to your husband will cause delays in what you want, financial mishaps, and messes that you have to help clean up, there are greater rewards. These rewards include

- Your husband will trust your heart and know that you are out for his good
- Your husband will be more apt to ask and heavily consider your advice in the future
- Your children will learn submission and humility from you
- God will bless you because of your obedience

There will be times in your life that you must function out of obedience and not convenience. Out of the right thing and not the easy thing. Many times the success of our Christian walk (and our marriage) is found in the times we do things that we don't want to do but know we should do.

This is a testament to our faith. Trusting that we don't have to always fix it or fight for it ourselves. Have the faith to believe that you don't have to live in defense mode with your husband. It is not up to you to "set the record straight," "make him see" or "put him in his place." Know that "God will fight for you; you need only to be still" (Exodus 14:14).

## Not Wrong, Just Different

If my husband and I meet at a location and have driven separate cars, it is our habit to try and beat the other one home. I am not sure when this competition started, but we do it every time. We both try to figure out the best route to take to beat the other person there. We give each other the stare down, and take off. Sometimes we will go the same route and hope that through smart and savvy maneuvering we can get ahead of the other person. Other times though, we take two completely different routes. Most times he wins but I am never far away. Most times it literally boils down to him turning in the driveway seconds before I do.

What I have learned by this game we play is that both my husband and I know multiple routes to get home and they are both just as quick and just as easy. In our marriages, many of the issues we have boil down to this as well. Many times there is no right or wrong, better or worse, but just his way and yours. So many of us need to say out loud that "His way is ok." Just that simple phrase may free you from unnecessary arguments and tension. Say this out loud three times: "His way is ok. His way is ok. His way is ok."

1 Peter 3:6 states that "Sarah obeyed her husband, Abraham, and called him Lord. You are her daughters when you do what is right without fear of what your husbands might do." This does not mean that we should elevate our husbands to the level of God in our lives because that would be the sin of idolatry. However, this does mean we should consider our husbands as "one having great power, authority or influence." Is this how you treat your husband?

## I Choose to Move

I don't have "road rage." Just a little "road attitude." For example, one of my worst road pet peeves is when a car is in the fast lane but not going *fast*. They look in their rearview mirror and see that they are obstructing the flow of traffic. But instead of getting over, they stand their ground and stay in that lane. Why? Because they have the right to be there. They have the right to be in that lane and everyone else will just have to adjust. They stay in that lane even though it causes frustration to the other drivers and causes others to make quick and irrational decisions.

Once when this happened to me, I whipped around a car and was just about to give them a little "road attitude," when the Lord stopped me in mid stare down. He convicted me by speaking these words to my spirit: "Many times in your household, you are that car that won't move."

He laid it on my heart that many times I have had the right to say something because it was true and it was my right to do so. But my household would have been much better served if I had chosen to remain silent.

Many times I have had the right to purchase something because "I work every day and I bring money into this household too," but what would it have done to my husband's view of me and my respect for him if I would have yielded to what he preferred. Many times I have had the right to say and do a lot of things, but it did not benefit my household or my marriage. So as wives I encourage and implore you that instead of fighting so hard for your rights, fight for your relationship. Many times that may mean choosing his preference over your pride, his desire over what you believe you deserve. And his need to be honored over your desire to be heard. So in your relationship, choose to "just move over."

Ponder:

If my husband has to check a box, would he view me as submissive or obstinate? Give three recent examples to support your answer.

*Acing Motherhood But Failing Marriage*

Pray:

Lord, give me the humility to submit. Decrease the desire to have things my way. Increase my ability to just say "OK." Help me to not confuse submission with weakness.

Practice:

For the next seven days, let your husband make all decisions, without any objection or modification from you. And *smile*.

## FACEBOOK FUNNIES:

So my 3 yr. old wanted to watch Nick Jr on my phone. So I tossed it to him. He said, "Mommy, don't throw it at me." and then hands it back to me and says, "Do it right." Checked by a 3 yr. old. Time to end this day. Good night Facebook

— May 8, 2013

CHAPTER 9

# *Facebook Fairy Tales*

*Where there is no guidance, the people fall, but in abundance of counselors there is victory. Proverbs 12:15*

Judging from Facebook, I and all of my 500 friends have fairy tale marriages. We flood our feed with date nights, vacations, Valentine's bouquets, and pictures of the pair of our feet on the beach. No one would ever know that behind the strategically posted pictures on Facebook, marriages are falling apart.

We will more often share our struggles with motherhood but are too embarrassed to share our marital issues. It is acceptable to have a mischievous child. It's ok to ask for parenting advice. But it's not ok to let anyone know you are having problems in your marriage. The willingness to share issues regarding motherhood create a strong support system and strong circle of counsel.

On the other hand, our inability to share our marital struggles causes us to suffer in silence. There is a stigma associated with having trouble in our marriage. So to avoid the stigma, we paint a picture that all is well, when in reality it's not. We ultimately crash and burn to the surprise of the 253 people that liked the photo of the two of you sharing a dessert posted just 2 days ago.

However, it is vital to the health of a marriage to have wise counsel and support from other people. Proverbs 15:22 says "Plans fail for lack of counsel, but with many advisers they succeed." One of the reasons marriages are failing at such an alarming rate is due to the lack of counsel.

Make it a priority to begin discussing with your husband, a safe network of people you both are comfortable using as mentors, accountability partners and advisors.

There has to be disclosure and agreement on who you establish these relationships with. If not, more division and harm could be the result.

Why these relationships are needed:

- ☐ Accountability – In every area of your life, especially marriage, you need to have someone who knows your goals, holds you to them and helps you achieve them.

- ☐ Advice – Many times a person not in the situation, can give great suggestions because they are seeing the situation from a different vantage point. They are not as emotionally invested as you and can think more rationally and wisely.

- ☐ Assistance – At times, you will need someone to actually come alongside and give physical, emotional, or financial assistance.

- ☐ Assurance – Hearing the words "you can get through this," "you are not alone" or "God has a plan for you. Hang in there," can give you a second wind to stay in the fight.

With whom do you seek to establish these relationships:

- ☐ Approved/Authorized – You and your spouse must agree who you can share issues with. You cannot share your issues with a random coworker at work because you feel comfortable with them. Or your sister, if your husband does not feel comfortable with that. If the two of you have not agreed to discuss certain matters with specific people, then your conversation with others about your marriage becomes inappropriate venting, not purposeful counsel. The purpose of any conversation you have with anyone else regarding your husband should have the heart of reconciliation at its core.

- ☐ Neutral – many times your mom, sister or best friend are not the best people to share your marital issues with. They are often unable to see past their love for you through to the real issue. They are usually biased and unhelpful. Remember, you are sharing your issues in order to resolve them, not just for sympathy. You also want to make sure the person will not take sides or hold grudges. Normally, our own family and friends are still angry with our spouses about an issue we have long since moved on from.

- ☐ Spiritually mature – You are seeking sound biblical advice, not someone's opinionated, worldly "two cents." Seek someone out that will not tell you what you want to hear, or what they think is right but the pure, untainted, truth in love.

- ☐ Experienced – I don't mean this in absolutes but primarily it should be with someone who is or has been married before. Some will argue that Jesus was not married and gave marriage advice. Please remember that he was the son of man and God and divine and all-knowing and omnipresent and omnipotent. Those criteria give him the street credit to speak on these issues. So with the exception of being divinity, someone who has experienced the highs and lows of marriage can relate well enough to provide accurate advice.

There is no shame in the fact that you do not have a perfect marriage. No one ever has or ever will. Trust that if you had a camera in the homes of the majority of married couples you would be shocked at the condition of their marriage. So seek the help others should be in search of as well.

What are my options?

*The couple* – There is a wonderful benefit to establishing a relationship with a couple you trust. It typically should not be a couple that has a close personal relationship with either spouse. Someone within the church, a coworker, or a couple recommended by someone else you trust. The key is to identify a couple with a heart for marriage who are both equally committed to the process.

There is no right or wrong set period of time, number of meetings, length of meetings or meeting format. Do what works with everyone's schedules. Do what is not forced or a burden. It might be once a month or once a week. It might also be dependent on the status of the relationship. If your issues are level 10 then maybe meeting more often is best. But if it is just for "maintenance work," infrequent but regularly scheduled meetings may be enough.

*The counselor* – Yep, I'm talking paid, professional, couch-laying counselor. Often times, it is healthy and necessary to get the expertise of a professional counselor to assist in navigating a successful marriage. The frequency of the sessions will vary based on the counselor's assessment of your individual and collective needs.

Remove any stigma you have surrounding seeing a counselor. Be more concerned about the health of your marriage than any preconceived notions you have.

*The crew* – It is a great idea to have a group of married couples the two of you spend time with regularly. Groups such as this provide fun, fellowship, natural accountability and perspective.

*The chosen one* – There should be one person that both you and your husband have to confide in. Your husband should have a male and you should have a female that supports each of you on this journey.

Titus 2:1-8 encourages teaching and training of one another. It would be wise for you as individuals to seek out someone who is in your life specifically to grow you in your areas of weakness and admonish you in areas where you are strong.

Ponder:

What couples, coworkers, friends, church or community leaders could be wise counsel to my husband and me? Make a list of names.

*Acing Motherhood But Failing Marriage*

Pray:

Lord, prepare my husband and me as we enter a season of vulnerability. Open us up to be receptive to counsel. Help us to discern who we can begin to establish relationships with in this area.

Practice:

Ask others to pray for you in certain areas of need. These may or may not be related to your marriage. Get comfortable with sharing the "not so perfect" areas of your life with trusted confidants.

## FACEBOOK FUNNIES:

I had a very hard day in a very hard week and my husband saw it all over my face and heard it all in my voice. I got home at 7pm to find a hot bubble bath and candle lit dinner waiting for me. Ya'll, I love this man.

— February 9, 2015

CHAPTER 10

# *I look better in 3D*

*He whose ear listens to the life giving reproof will dwell among the wise. Proverbs 15:31*

Three D movies are becoming increasingly more popular. Production companies have realized that consumers will pay more money on already overpriced tickets in order to have the 3D experience. We enjoy the action flying off the screen. It makes the action seem bigger, brighter and better.

You may have never been on the big screen, but more than likely your children are looking at you in 3D. They believe we can fix, explain, and handle anything. They view us through their beautifully biased mommy lenses. In their eyes, we are the best, biggest, brightest, and most brilliant person they know.

It is great that our children think we are Super Mom. There is security in believing that mom has everything under control. Younger kids should think we know how clouds are formed, that we can scare the closet monsters away, bake their favorite cake, and magically find their missing shoe. Teenagers need to feel that mom can convince the chemistry teacher to offer a retest, negotiate with the car salesman to give them a reduced price on their first car, and knows all the steps to correctly completing a college application.

As our children navigate through a confusing and cruel world, they need to have full confidence in mommy's ability to get them through it. Our children's confidence in us creates an environment in which most of us thrive. These feelings of validation and encouragement inspire us. We work harder to figure things out for them. We team up with them against any opposition and fight hard to conquer it. We go to great lengths to daily earn the title of Super Mom.

Unfortunately, time and truth have broken our husbands' 3D lenses, replacing them with a magnifying glass. Over the years, our husbands have developed the ability to see all of our blemishes and faults that others may not know exist.

They have seen us at some of our lowest points and at our worst behavior. Even beyond what many of our closest friends and family have seen, our spouses have witnessed the pieces of us that others would be shocked to know we possess.

He has seen the unchecked anger you lash at him with. He has caught you in lies that your friends would be amazed you told. He has overheard your nightly gossipy conversations with your best friend. He has observed the jealousy you have towards your sister. He knows your shortcomings, mistakes, character flaws and sins. He knows that perfectly groomed, high heel wearing, dessert baking, deal closing, jovial woman you portray to the world is also the same sleep bonnet wearing, foot odor battling, cookie burning, last minute procrastinating, stressed out woman you are behind closed doors.

There is difficulty in relating to someone who knows you completely for who you are and not who you want to be. Feelings of vulnerability, judgment and defensiveness can swell up if you are not careful.

You have been exposed and it's okay. Your assets draw him to you but your growth opportunities keep him connected. Ironically enough, your imperfections give him purpose in your life. Your husband wants to be able to help you in ways beyond fixing the broken toilet and unscrewing the top off of a jar. Your husband needs to feel that you go to him and not always your friend for advice. He wants to be the person you discuss the pros and cons of possibly switching jobs. When you are emotionally drained, he needs to know that you look to him for

*Acing Motherhood But Failing Marriage*

encouragement.

Men are task oriented and goal driven. If you do not give him a purpose in your life, he will check out and not have much concern for you as an individual.

In what areas of your life have you sought your husband's help? When was the last time you asked his opinion on a personal matter? The last time he offered a specific critique of you, did you shut him down or open up and listen. As your husband sees he is needed for your emotional, professional, physical and spiritual wellbeing, he will take a greater responsibility for those. Some of you may be quick to say that you can handle these alone and don't want him overly involved. Trust me, you want your husband vested in these areas.

If he feels you always "got it," he won't offer to help you. Then you will most likely become discouraged and frustrated because "he is never there for you." When the truth is, you "had it" and didn't need him, so he stopped offering.

You can't have it both ways. I am not suggesting you act as a damsel in distress who cannot help herself. I am suggesting though, that you leave enough room in your life that he is needed to help you. He needs to hear you say, "Can you help me with this?" "What do you think?" "I have been waiting all day to get your opinion on this." Needing your husband is much deeper than the "honey do" list you make each Saturday morning. Needing your husband looks like creating an environment where it is clear that you are dependent on him in many life areas.

Did I say the awful "D" word? Dependence. Almost more dreaded than the "S" word. Submission. Men want to feel needed, relied upon. Yes, long legs, flowing hair and high heels are attractive to men. Equally as attractive is a woman who needs him and lets him know it. In our culture, we have been taught that self-sufficiency creates security. In marriage, too much self-sufficiency creates separation. An increase in independence decreases intimacy. When you seek autonomy in marriage, what you will ultimately find is agitation. As I drive to work, I often wonder why there aren't more people using the high-occupancy vehicle (HOV) lane. As I sit frustrated and at a standstill, it irritates me to see cars to my left zooming past. I, like most Americans, don't want to be bothered with the hassle of coordinating my schedule with another person, the inconvenience of having to wait on someone, and not having the ability to come and go based on what works best for me. So we trade the ability to move through traffic faster and get to work sooner, for the ability to "do it our way." As it is in many marriages. We choose the frustrations of being stuck in certain life situations just to be able to say, I am doing this my way.

Is it worth it? Why not hop in the HOV lane? What if you laid aside some of your desire to be self-sufficient in order to move through life with your husband at a much smoother pace? What would happen if you stopped projecting "I got it" and starting asking "what do you think?"

Ponder:

Does it make you uncomfortable that your husband knows all your mess and mistakes? Do you feel embarrassed, ashamed, or exposed in some situations by your husband? Do you believe this has affected how the two of you interact?

Pray:

Lord, give me the confidence to be comfortable with the truth that both good and bad live in me. Allow me to take my husband's hand to help me be better.

Practice:

At least once a day for a week, ask your husband's opinion on a decision you need to make. Also, at least once a week, ask your husband's opinion on something you did or said.

## FACEBOOK FUNNIES:

(Posted By Eric) Are men supposed to get anything for Valentine's Day? I'm asking for my wife. #Ididntgetnuttin

## CHAPTER 11

# *Enough brownie points should earn brownies*

*A gift opens the way and ushers the giver into the presence of the great. Proverbs 18:16*

I was singing the "Clean up" song. You know it. "Clean up, clean up, everybody everywhere, clean up, clean up, everybody do your share." My baby girl would find anything she could physically pick up and one by one bring each item to me. As quickly as her little legs could carry her, she brought a shoe, a fork, pieces of paper or a pair of pants (Don't judge me. Yes, all of these things are often on my floor at one time. I said we were cleaning, didn't I?). Once she put it in my hand, I would clap and say "thank you." Then I would kiss her and tell her how nice and helpful she was. If I allowed it, it would have gone on for hours. Why? Because when I recognized and rewarded her behavior, she desired to do it again and again.

Many times I specifically seek ways to positively reinforce behavior that I want my children to repeat. This is also known as "treats." Chocolate for Danielle. Action figures for Yuriah. Money for Kaden. I know what makes my kiddos tick and when appropriate, I reward them using the things they enjoy.

We give our children treats to reinforce behavior but just expect our husbands to do right for right's sake. Yes, they should. But do they? As Dr. Phil would say, "And how is that working for you?" A counselor once told me that if you like something your husband did, recognize it and say thank you, or he won't do it again. Simply put, recognize what you want repeated.

Is there a behavior you need from your husband that he does not do at all or often enough? Then reward him when he does it, no matter how infrequent it is. Does your husband have an irritating habit that you desperately want stopped? The next time he refrains, make a big deal out of it. You can be stubborn and refuse to reward him based off your argument of "He is supposed to do that anyway!" However, it will not get you anywhere. Know how to play the game or continue to fight an uphill, losing battle.

*Training the Dragon that Shares your Bed*

There was a Disney movie called "How to Train Your Dragon." Despite having three children, I somehow missed seeing this one. But I find the title intriguing. The title indicates that there is a specific technique for "training" something that is seemingly impossible to tame. Ladies, if you want to train your dragon, do it with consistent and relevant rewards. By consistent, I mean often enough to keep him wanting more. By relevant, I mean things he likes.

Whether it be cooking his favorite meal, offering a back rub, telling him to go have fun with his friends instead of accompanying you to Chuck E. Cheese for the neighbor kid's birthday party. Whatever hits home for him, give it to him.

*The Treat of Touch*

My youngest son and I Eskimo kiss quite often. My older son, a little too cool for lots of mommy affection, will occasionally lay across my lap as I rub his head. When my baby girl is sleepy I love rocking and rubbing her until she falls into a deep slobbery sleep. I enjoy kissing, hugging, rubbing and holding my children. They rarely have to ask me. I just offer it.

I understand this connects us. Touching my children shows them know how much I care for them. It also fills me with a sense of validation, comfort and affirmation.

If I understand that physical touch brings connectedness, intimacy and strengthens bonds, then why is it so difficult to share this with my husband consistently? Why am I excited to reward my children with physical touch, but irritated when my husband asks?

When he asks me to rub his head, I immediately think "When was the last time you rubbed me?" My need for reciprocity hinders me from rewarding my husband in this way.

Don't withhold physical touch from your husband in any capacity for any reason. Rub his head. Give him a massage. Give him a pedicure.

*SEX!*

And yes, sex falls under physical touch as well. Rocking your daughter to sleep may be all she needs, but your husband needs more than that.

I honestly believe that most women could have sex 12 times a year (about once a month) and be ok. Most of us enjoy sex just enough to have it on a random and infrequent basis. Mainly due to the fact we just don't think about it.

Men, on the other hand, think about sex daily, several times a day. I compare this to an adult and a child's appetite. Most young children don't eat much. Mainly because their small stomachs fill up quickly but also because food is low on their priority list. Seeing what mischief they can get into is much more fun. When they do eat, it's not much.

What if children thought we were barbaric gluttons for eating as often and as much as we do? Would their perception of us be correct? Of course not. The requirements of food for children and adults are completely different.

The same is true for men as it relates to sex. Their bodies want it more than we do, but it is still very natural. If we judge them based on our appetite for sex, we will unfairly label them as sex crazed perverts.

*SEX SEX SEX*

Say it with me. SEX. SEX. SEX. Many women don't like talking much about it, especially Christian women. We have been taught that sex is at worse, bad or at a minimum, not ladylike.

We have to get comfortable with the notion that mother, Children's Church leader, friendly neighbor and awesome sex partner can live in the same body. We have to be comfortable with shopping on Amazon for La La Lucy for your daughter and lingerie for your husband. We should confidently step to the grocery store register with Orajel for our little baby and warming gel for our big baby. The same woman that shops for toddler toys should not be embarrassed to buy sex toys. Ladies, there is no contrast in being a mother and a lover.

A blogger friend of mine, Christen Jacobs, wrote "Many people have an unbiblical view that God is somehow against sex. God is in fact the creator of sex. It is a gift that he has given to the husband and wife not only for the purpose of procreation but for the purpose of pleasure."

Sex is not wrong; it is right. It is not nasty; it is pure. It is not a guilty pleasure; it should be complete pleasure. Get comfortable with sharing this form of touch and intimacy with your husband.

Talk about it with your husband as well. We have no shortage of words expressing what we need from him but when it comes to one of his primary needs, we close up like a clam. We have to discuss frequency, positions, preferences and experiment with our man. The ability to have candid discussion regarding sex with your spouse will transform the experience for both of you.

So begin this week having regular sex (the definition of regular will vary per couple). Even if you have to set a calendar reminder. No, this is not overkill, because sex is something that connects you to him and him to you. It must not be neglected or underestimated.

Every week set a reminder to initiate sex. Yes, *you* initiate it. Make him feel attractive, wanted and desired. Take note of how expressing that you want him, makes him want you.

Set another reminder weekly that says massage. Then set a daily reminder that says rub his head or back. Do this until it becomes second nature.

Physical touch—both sexual and non-sexual—may not be your love language. What does not come naturally, must be planned and scheduled. A simple way to think about sex is like drinking water. You don't have to be thirsty to drink water because you realize the health benefits of water. We do not let the feeling of thirst act as our only indicator light to hydrate our bodies. We also use our knowledge of our bodies need for water, even in the absence of the physical craving, to give our bodies what is needed. The same is true of sex. Don't wait until you are desiring sex before you joyfully respond to his initiation or initiate yourself. Provide him what he needs, not solely based on your own physical desire, but on your knowledge of the need.

*No Transfer Accepted*

Sorry ladies, no transfers. The only thing that will satisfy his need for sex, is sex. The spotless kitchen does not satisfy this. The two hours of car pool you successfully handled today does not count here. Your hard day at the office, the closet you organized or your trip to the doctor with his mom cannot be transferred to this account. So don't get upset with him when after your hard day, he still has the audacity to ask for sex.

If you were in school and worked diligently to prepare a 100-page research paper for English would you argue with the Algebra teacher that he needed to cut you some slack in class because of the English assignment. Sorry ladies. English does not count for Algebra. Neither do your other responsibilities at home and work count towards sex.

Ponder:

Make a list of five material things your husband likes. Make another list of five non-tangible things he enjoys that you do for him. Make sure you have a clear and accurate understanding of appropriate rewards for your husband.

Pray:

Lord, give me the humility to reward. Allow my husband to be validated and uplifted by my relevant rewards.

Practice:

Pick a reward from your list each time he does something you appreciate. Notice and journal the response.

## FACEBOOK FUNNIES:

Thanks Eric Rollins for a quick random weeknight date. Gone for less than 2 hrs. No reservations or anything major but good conversation and laughs with my baby.

— Jan 15, 2015

CHAPTER 12

## *Pump Him Up*

*Therefore encourage one another and build each other up. 1 Thessalonians 5:11*

"Go, baby! Come on. You can do it, big boy. I know you can! Mommy is going to be so proud of you." These words rolled off my tongue as naturally and swiftly as water from a leaf. At least 10 times a day during this season of my son's life, I would fill his ears and his head with so much encouragement. I made songs about how much I believed in his potential. I danced and I clapped to push him on to success. I bragged about him to friends, family and perfect strangers in his presence so he would know just how proud I was of him. I consistently asked him how he was doing in this area and if I could help. I reminded him. Assisted him. Reassured him. I wanted him to know how important his endeavor was to me. I made it known with my words and my deeds that I was his biggest supporter. All of this from me just so he would pee in a commode. Yep, I was his proud potty-training cheerleader.

Whether potty training, learning the alphabet, a completed pass in football, learning to walk, or an A on a test, I naturally encourage my children. As I write this, I am seeing image after image of me clapping, jumping up and down, picking them up to hug them, and speaking well of them to friends and family. All in the name of encouragement. The images are vivid and numerous.

However, as I sit and think about times I encourage my husband, the video reel of images is much harder to recall. I can think of sporadic instances of verbal encouragement to my husband but they pale in comparison to those of my children.

I encourage my children as a lifestyle. I encourage my husband as an event.

I speak words of affirmation to my children without thought or effort because I realize they need it. My children need my encouragement for the following reasons:

- ☐ They are unsure of themselves and I want to increase their confidence.

- ☐ Peers can tear them down and I want to build them back up.

- ☐ Failures and delays discourage them and I want to insure they won't quit.

Maybe this is the great disconnect with encouraging our husbands. We don't realize they need our encouragement for the same reasons. The need for encouragement exists in our spouses just as deeply as it does in our children.

*Our husbands can be unsure of themselves*

Just like our children, our men are unsure of themselves in many situations. Their confidence in themselves wavers at a new job, making a presentation for the first time, during parenting, or while leading their household. Many times they won't admit it out of pride. Other times they don't realize their own uncertainties. In either case, they will rarely ask for encouragement or show clear signs they need it. As wives, we have to stay tuned in well enough to know the need, even if not expressed. Always, in every situation, assume the need. Don't wait to be asked. Don't wait to see him cry, struggle or fall. Assume the need to encourage, always. Your words can literally shape how your husband views himself. So make sure those words are encouraging.

*Peer Pressure*

*Acing Motherhood But Failing Marriage*

Many times when we think of peers, we automatically think of children or teenagers. As adults, we have peers as well. We also have peer pressure, peer influences and we care about what our peers think of us.

As our husbands interact with people at work, friends, other husbands, family and the world at large, they are judged, criticized and graded on their performance. Oftentimes, this pressure leads to a feeling of being torn down. We must step in to build them back up. We are the refueling station for our husbands' empty tanks. This role, if taken seriously, can energize our husbands and our households beyond belief.

*Defeats and Delays Discourage*

Men thrive on success and results. When there is a lack of either one of these, they get discouraged. As wives, we can be a great influence on whether they quit or keep pushing. They could quit a multitude of things including their jobs, interacting with their children, or the marriage. Our words and deeds of affirmation can "hold them over" until they see results.

*Getting Past the Awkwardness*

Due to the dynamic of a husband/wife relationship brought on by any number of factors, it is often uncomfortable and undesirable to some wives to compliment and encourage their husbands. If a husband is harsh with his wife, then it will make it difficult for her to encourage him. If there is tension because of a husband's poor money management, then it will be difficult to encourage him in other areas. What you must acknowledge, accept and act on is that the need still exists even in the presence of discomfort or lack of desire.

You are a cheerleader. Cheerleaders do not get the option to only cheer during a winning season. A good cheerleader doesn't put down her pom-poms and sit with the crowd and boo when her team is down. A great cheerleader actually cheers harder and with more intensity when her team is behind. As the cheer captain for your husband, at no point is it acceptable to stop cheering for him. No matter how deep your marital issues are, you must find areas of authentic encouragement and speak those to him.

If some of us told the complete truth, we would admit we don't want our husbands knowing we think well of them. That sounds insane to say, but in speaking with many wives I know this to be a fact. Many times the discord in a marriage has gotten to a point of dislike or distain for a spouse. So even if a wife recognizes the need, the need goes unfulfilled, because she does not want to build her husband up. We feel that he doesn't deserve our compliments or affirmation. At this point, the wife is in sin and wrong. If you are still in the marriage, then perform as such. Put your "big girl pants" on underneath your skirt, pick up the pom-poms and mega phone and get to cheering him on.

We also have to say thank you and celebrate him for things that he should be doing anyway. Yes, say thank you when he picks up his underwear. I know this is something he is supposed to do. Still, say thank you. When he helps get the kids ready in the morning, tell him you appreciate it. Yes, he should have helped you a long time ago. Still say thank you. Yes, he should go to work and provide for your family, and help around the house, and pray with you. But whenever he does it, tell him how great he is at it and that you appreciate it.

For those of you that need a little assistance, here are some examples:

1. You have been working very long hours at work and coming home extremely tired. Thank you for still making time to help with the kids' homework when you get here. That really helps me out.

2. Your bonus came! You did a great job this quarter. I know you have been stressed out with work, but your hard work paid off. Good job.

3. Baby, you look good today. You have been working out just two weeks but it is showing already.

4. I know Justin's behavior has not gotten much better at school, but I see you working so hard to help him. I appreciate you being so involved with our son and I know he will come around because of you.

*The Extra Step*

Encouragement is not just lip service. Our actions have to supplement our words. What are you *doing* that shows you believe in and support your husband? Let's take the above examples a step further.

1. You have been working very long hours at work and coming home extremely tired. Thank you for still making time to help with the kids' homework when you get here. That really helps me out. I've ironed your clothes for the week, so you can sleep a little later the next few mornings. And you know I hate ironing.

2. Your bonus came! You did a great job this quarter. I know you have been stressed out with work, but your hard work paid off. Good job. I remember you mentioned that an iPad would help you get things done when you were traveling, so I bought you one.

3. Baby, you look good today. You have been working out just two weeks but it is showing already. I know you have been struggling to find time to work out, so I don't mind you coming home a little later on Tuesdays and Thursdays. I can handle the kids while you go to the gym.

4. I know Justin's behavior has not gotten much better at school, but I see you working so hard to help him. I appreciate you being so involved with our son and I know he will come around because of you. I want to make sure that I am in line with how

you are disciplining him. Is there something you see that I can be doing differently with him?

*Redo the Ratio*

I have often been discouraged by my husband's reaction after I expressed something I wanted him to do differently. On several occasions I have expressed a criticism or concern that sent him into what I felt was "victim mode." He has labeled me as a nag, being negative, or not ever being encouraging. I would stand there utterly confused and defeated because I could recount several times that I had expressed good things towards him and even been intentional about it. I often would feel that he only remembered the negative things I would say and not ever remember or appreciate my words of encouragement.

Dr. John Cacioppo of the University of Chicago has put a name to this all too familiar and frustrating phenomenon. He says that our brain has a "negativity bias." Negatives imprint and stick in our memories much quicker and longer than positives. Our minds are more sensitive and responsive to the bad and the ugly, rather than the good. This fully explains why expressing frustration that my husband never cleans out the bathtub when he is done, negates the five times I thanked him for helping me with laundry.

The unfortunate reality is that our brain absorbs negative information like water in a large and super absorbent sponge but positive information like a pitcher of water being poured into a thimble. Every critique or concern you express, even if true and valid, is like making an emotional withdrawal. So for every one negative statement we make, we have to make sure there have been 10 more positive deposits. Have you deposited enough in your husband's affirmation account?

Also, understand that each deposit is worth the same amount. Don't think that one big expression of gratitude will fill a depleted account. It is the frequency and not the size of the deposits that matter most.

For example, have you ever scoffed at a husband who thought purchasing his wife an expensive birthday gift and dinner at a fine restaurant would improve their deteriorating marriage. You understood that one big deposit could not make up for his *daily* negative behavior and remarks.

Or at a wife who purchased a surprise airline ticket for her husband to go visit his best friend thinking it would compensate for her continual nagging and critical comments.

One super-size positive *cannot* offset multiple negatives. Remember, the frequency of the positive is what matters most.

*What not to say!*

"There is one who speaks rashly like the thrusts of a sword but the tongue of the wise brings healings" (Proverbs 12:18).

"Death and life are in the power of the tongue" (Proverbs 18:21).

"The soothing tongue is a tree of life but a perverse tongue crushes the spirit" (Proverbs 15:4).

Encouragement is not just what you say. It is also what you refrain from saying. Oftentimes our words bring strong discouragement to our spouses. We must be slow to speak (James 1:19) in order to stop ourselves from being discouraging in our speech.

In an article in Woman's Day Online by Denise Schipani she lists *10 things you should never say to your kids*. This article was designed to help preserve and protect a child's self-esteem. I have made a list of ten things you should never say to your husband. My list seeks to protect your husband's ego and manhood.

1. "My ex used to…" – Never compare your husband to anyone, especially not to someone you were in a past relationship with. Though men are competitive, that competitive nature does not apply to "The Ghost of Boyfriends Past." Comparing them to

your ex is insulting and embarrassing. They won't compete against this.

2. "You never ..." – Never use absolutes (oh wait, I just did). Words like "never," "always," "all," and "none" need to be used very sparingly in conversations with your spouse. First of all, when you speak in absolutes you are rarely being truthful. Most often absolutes are emotional exaggerations. Second, if your husband feels you have overlooked something he has done or has been working on, he will likely stop trying. So if you say "you are never romantic" and he bought you flowers last month, then I hope you took a picture of them because those may be the last you'll get for a long while. Even if that is the only romantic thing he has done in months, he counts it as a valiant effort and you just let him know you didn't think much of his effort.

3. "I always ..." – Again, never use absolutes, even when referring to yourself. Your husband does not want you to paint yourself as the heroine or the victim. When you say "I am the only one who ever ...," you become a prideful heroine or a whinny victim. Neither are attractive to a man. More importantly, neither will encourage him to change his behavior, because he will feel there is little truth and more exaggeration of your own perception.

4. "This is just how I am." – We often hide behind this as a way to say "how can you expect me to change something that is woven into the very fiber of my being?" when it is usually something we can change, but we don't want to put in the work to do so. Your husband does not want to hear the thing that puts a barrier between him emotionally connecting with you will never improve.

5. "Just let me do it." – When a man feels that his efforts are not appreciated because you think you can do it better, he will not

*Acing Motherhood But Failing Marriage*

be likely to help you with that or any other tasks. Men hate micromanagement. Men also hate being given instructions and directions if they have not asked for them. They also resent a "know it all" spirit, especially in women. If you want your man to be more of an initiator of things that need to be done in your household, then do not jump in and take over anything he is doing. Even if it means that it will take longer or not be done 100 percent correctly.

6. "I'll do it but I don't like it." – Attitude is everything, ladies. If he asks you to watch football with him and you say yes, but you list a thousand other things that need to be done, then you might as well go do those thousand other things. You just spoiled it! If you are going to do something your husband asks of you, know that *how* you do it is just as important.

7. "Can't you just do it yourself?" – If he asks you, then he wants you to do it, or he would not have asked. It might be because of his inability, time or convenience. Whatever the reason, he asked you.

8. "I would rather ask someone else." – Be careful not to elevate others over your husband by suggesting others are better at something that your husband has stepped up to do. There are times; however, when he has to be reined in because the results could be catastrophic. For example if your husband who has never used a power tool in this life suggests that he can bust up the tile in your bathroom and lay the new wood floors on this own. This might be a time to have a gentle discussion suggesting he hire a professional. However, most times men want to try things that are within realistic realms of what they can do. Let them try.

9. "I don't care what you do." – Don't say what you don't mean. If you give your husband permission to do what he wants, not considering your wants or needs and he does it, then you are

partly to blame. You don't ever want to give your husband permission to disregard you.

10. "I told you so." – Men hate being wrong. They despise others knowing they were wrong. They loathe a woman being right about what they were wrong about. Because they hate it so much, they take note of it. So they don't need you to.

Be aware of the fact that negativity is natural. Which means that saying discouraging things will roll off your tongue faster than the time it takes you to bite your bottom lip. Therefore, you have to pray and practice. Pray for the ability to exercise the spirit of wisdom and kindness in your speech. Practice being slow to speak. Forcing yourself to think before you speak is one of the wisest practices you can possibly implement.

Words are like branding. When first said they are immeasurably painful. Over time, with treatment and attention, the pain and scars heal. However, there is always a reminder that forever alters the state of the relationship. How are you branding/permanently altering your relationship with your husband with your choice of words?

Also, try saying more with less. If we want our words to carry more impact with our husbands, we need to be as clear, concise and thorough as possible. The only way you can successfully do this is to practice and plan. Whenever possible plan what you are going to say before actually saying it. This way you can edit and delete, giving him only the final draft.

As an author, the version of the book that you are reading is much different than what I initially sent to my editor. Along with grammatical and punctuation corrections, my editor deleted many words, sentences and even entire paragraphs. At first I was offended and defensive. All I could see was the eloquence of my words being lost. Her consistent response to me was less is more. In essence she wanted me to keep the words that pack a punch and delete the fluff. I caution you to be your own editor in conversations with your husband.

### Broadening your Definition of Respect

One of the most popular and prudent verses of scripture related to marriage is Ephesians 5:33, "Each individual among you also is to love his own wife even as himself, and the wife must see to it that she respects her husband." Do you respect your husband? Before you quickly answer, consider that the most common definition of respect we apply to this verse is feeling or showing deferential regard. This definition means not yelling, being agreeable, not going behind his back doing something that he would not have you do and other things of that nature. Many of you would say that you do a good job of respect using that definition.

As wives, I believe that we neglect another component of respect. A broader definition of respect is to admire someone deeply as a result of their abilities, qualities or achievements. Do you respect your husband in that way? When was the last time you thought about the great things your husband has done? His accomplishments at work, his relationship with his kids, his charm with people or his intelligence. When was the last time you took note of what a good guy he is? Reestablish respect for the good things about your husband. Once you do this, voice them to him.

To help you understand respect more deeply, reflect on the following synonyms:

Respect:

Reverence

Honor

Consider

Prefer

Esteem

Value

Put first

Many of us do not show respect (yelling, cursing or negative communication or actions) for our husbands because we have lost respect (deep admiration) for them. Despite his faults, you must find and concentrate on the things you respect about him. Once you do this, encouraging him will become second nature.

Ponder:

Make a list of all the things you respect (admire) about your husband.

Pray:

Lord, help me to rebuild the respect for my husband by focusing on his areas of greatness and uniqueness. Allow this focus to manifest in greater respect in my behavior.

Practice:

Every day this week verbally esteem your husband.

## FACEBOOK FUNNIES:

Riding with my husband while he is on a business call with one of his employees. Watching him manage is kind of sexy. #lovehim #attractedtohim #makethatmoneyboo

CHAPTER 13

## *Till Death (or something like it) Do Us Part*

*A wife is bound to her husband as long as he lives. 1 Corinthians 7:39*

My aunt and I often joke that we are not just ladies, but "lady-ladies." When she and I refer to someone as just a lady, that simply identifies the gender. But when we say a "lady-lady," that means a child rearing, job holding, bill paying, "shol nuf" adult women. We joke with one another about the stresses and responsibilities of being a "lady-lady."

Even though I have reached "lady-lady" status, that does not deter my mom from calling to make sure I made it home in the rain, lecturing me about wearing a jacket when the temperature dips anywhere below 75, reminding me to set the security system and sending multiple Tupperware containers full of food home with me. Why does she still do this even after I have long since moved from under her roof? Because I will always be her baby. She desires to still fill her role as mother no matter my age. When she gave birth to me, she made the decision to be mommy, forever.

I'm sure you are no different. As mothers, the past, present and future of our children compel us to act and respond. Have you recently sent your child living away at college a care package of things you assume they need? Did you offer to babysit your grandkids because you figured your daughter was tired from a long work week? Are you saving to help your child with tuition, their wedding, or first home? Despite the age of our "babies," we are still committed to walking this life journey with them. Motherhood never ends. Motherhood never takes breaks. Motherhood is simply forever.

Do you see marriage in the same light? Sure, you repeated those words at the wedding. Yes, you still say it now. But do you fundamentally believe it to the core. Do your actions point to the fact that you have decided to be his life partner forever?

Do you have a secret bank account, just in case he leaves? Or is every dollar of your household income combined? Have you accepted invitations from your girlfriends to "come stay with me if you ever need a place to go?" (when it was not due to an issue of safety) Or do you lovingly but firmly rebuke them for suggesting divorce as an option? Do you spend time daydreaming of what it would be like to be single again? Or do you take every thought captive and command your thoughts to concentrate on ways to mend your marriage?

Much higher than just agreeing to be legally bound to your husband until death parts you two, have you decided to be his friend, lover and partner forever. Maybe a better question is have you decided to be committed to living a healthy and progressive relationship with your husband forever? Not just sharing a house but making a home. Greater than sharing bank accounts, but mutually working on your financial futures. Not just sticking it out, but building it up.

When your children are unlikable, never do you consider disowning them. Typically, when your children's bad behaviors rise, so does your intensity to rescue them. However, when our husbands' bad behavior increases, many times we seek an exit rather than a way to bring him back around.

You are your husband's life partner. Which means you made an agreement with him to live the rest of your days on earth strengthening your union, not just being present. Just showing up for a game never accomplished any victory. You have to get on the field and bring your A game, every day.

The only way you truly develop a forever mindset is by making that decision every single day. So, what did yesterday look like? If I had a camera that followed you around yesterday, would it be obvious you were committed to sharing your lifetime with him or would it appear that you checked out. Daily we must live with forever in mind. Every day ask yourself this question, "What can I do today that will get us to forever?"

With forever in mind, we won't stay angry long. Because at some point we will reason with ourselves that if we are going to be with this guy for the next 60 years, what does staying mad at him for the next 2 days accomplish? With forever in mind, we would rather cook for him than have him eating out often because we would rather have a healthy 75-year-old than an unhealthy one. With forever in mind, the little things matter less, the big things take precedence.

The forever mindset forces us to make smart decisions. Stubbornness, silent treatments, dishonestly winning, and keeping score will seem rather trivial. Those are battles. We are going for the war victory.

Though we see the world getting divorced at startling rates, don't buy into the lie that marriage is something you quit when it doesn't feel good anymore. Excessive arguing is not a reason to get divorced. Being "just so different" isn't either. Differing opinions about money is not a deal breaker. In Christ, there is no such thing as irreconcilable differences. Marriage is forever, not until you "feel you can't do it anymore."

A good friend of mine Shenequa Bailey Cager said this on her Facebook page, That Wife Life:

"Tough seasons in a marriage suck! It's so isolating! Who do you tell? How do you bounce back? Do you leave? Do you stay? Trying to pray but have no words? Trying to be cordial but to no avail! Feeling like a sucka! Feeling played! Feeling guilty! Feeling numb! Wanna hug him! Wanna slap him? Tough seasons in a marriage suck!

Oh I don't have a fix. Sorry! I'm just a wife who can simply say...

You're not alone. God really hasn't forgotten you. Yes, it hurts like hell! Don't trust your emotions; they will deceive and betray you! God didn't make a mistake and even this is a part of your destiny! Reach out to a friend/confidant! Cry! Throw a fit!

And then…Put your clothes on and press on, trusting God!"

Don't grow weary in well doing. There will be times that you are doing everything right. Fulfilling him sexually, being respectful, light-hearted and kind and your husband is being mean, evil and hard to get along with. Even during these times, continue doing what you know is right, even when you are not getting the results you want.

Ponder:

Does the thought of being married to your husband for the next 50 years sound encouraging or scary? If it sounds encouraging, then celebrate the reasons why. Actually take inventory of those great things about your husband and your relationship.

If it sounds scary, then make a list of the three big reasons why.

Pray:

Lord, give me the strength, desire, and resolve to make it to forever.

Practice:

Take the three "scary" reasons above and get help. Talk to your husband. Commit to counseling. Pray! Make a specific plan to tackle these issues head-on beginning today.

# FACEBOOK FUNNIES:

Sometimes I take for granted that my husband wants to be around me and hang out with me. To many, that may sound like a small thing, but it's not. Thanks Eric Rollins for both loving and LIKING me. #ontherunsinceNov2006

— Aug 2. 2014

## CHAPTER 14:

# *Fishing, Football, and Fried Food*

*Be devoted to one another in love. Honor one another above yourselves. Romans 12:10*

I allowed my oldest to lure me onto a rollercoaster, even though I swore off them years ago. I risked my equilibrium and life solely because I wanted to share this fun experience with my son.

Even though it was into the lower 70s outside, my son wanted to get in the pool and I obliged. I emptied my pockets and jumped in the pool fully clothed because I wanted to give my son a random fun highlight in an otherwise routine day.

Despite the pain in my wobbly legs from giving my daughter pony rides, I continued to bounce my daughter as high as my wobbly legs would launch her. Her uncontrollable laughter was like music to my soul.

Whether a walk to the park, jumping outside on the trampoline, going skating or go-kart riding, I am constantly looking for ways to ensure my children have a good time in life. Even typical moments around the house are filled with intentional moments of fun. I have initiated Nerf gun fights, baked cookies at midnight and snow-ball fights in the dead of winter, all in the name of fun.

The realization that one day my kids will have to be responsible for bills, deadlines, and other adult duties compels me to bring as much fun into their lives now as possible. What I often forget is that my husband has to daily focus on bills, deadlines, and major responsibilities. I should feel a greater compulsion to fill his life with fun that carries him through the daily grind of adulthood.

Our husbands need to have fun, too. As wives we often stress to our husbands the need to grow up, but what if having fun is just as important to their wellbeing.

What if the massage you so desperately need is the equivalent for him to a flag football game with his friends? The day of retail therapy that excites you is no more important than the video games he loves. The long conversations you have with your girlfriend recharge you the way going to a high school football game with his friend does for him.

So the next time you have the urge to tell him to stop wrestling with your son because he has homework, resist it. Bite your tongue the next time you want to chastise him for wrapping you in the sheet like a mummy instead of folding it. When he wants to skip grocery shopping and go bike riding, oblige him.

Each of our husbands' heart has a small Peter Pan's living inside. (I just saw an image of my husband in green leotards and a feather in his hat. Absolutely hilarious!) They want to have the occasional opportunity to live in "Neverland" before they have to return to the realities of the real world. Let them!

Play is not just for kids. Psychologists have written entire books about the importance of play for adults. Julie Baumgardner, a Certified Family Life Educator says, "studies show that a life lived without play is at increased risk for stress-related diseases, mental health issues, addiction and interpersonal violence."

According to the National Institute of Health, "Play is the gateway to vitality. By its nature it is uniquely and intrinsically rewarding. It generates optimism, seeks out novelty, makes perseverance fun, leads to mastery, gives the immune system a bounce, fosters empathy and promotes a sense of belonging and community. Each of these play by-products are indices of personal health, and their shortage predicts impending health problems and personal fragility."

Allowing your husband play time can positively impact your relationship and his health.

Be his buddy and his friend. Join him in the fun of life. Be his playmate. Many times we get upset that our husbands do not like spending time with us. Why don't they? Could it be they don't view us as fun and would rather be with their friends? That could be a hard truth to swallow. If that is your truth, make the choice now to create an environment that makes him want to be with you.

Your husband loves the fact that you can cook great meals, keep a clean house, and keep the kids organized. None of those reasons; however, are why he married you. He married you because he connected with you and had fun with you.

Think about TV or movie relationships that you love to watch develop. I personally love the relationship between Clair and Heathcliff Huxtable (The Cosby Show), Jill and Tim Taylor (Tool Time) and Martin and Gina Lawrence (Martin). These relationships were full of life, love and laughter. I know that real life is not a scripted sitcom with a team of professional writers, but real life can be full of funny moments. Write your own story daily. Choose to pencil in laughter and fun despite the struggles and stress the day brings.

Encourage that fun spirit in your husband. Don't choke it out of him. Many times it is the men that bring the excitement element to our homes. Yes, our children need the structure that we bring, but they also need the spice for life that our husbands most naturally provide.

*Do What He Wants To Do*

My oldest son loves sports. He is really into football and basketball. By into, I mean obsessed. If he is not sleeping, he is practicing his jumper or a run route. I have never been good at basketball and therefore have had little to no interest in playing it. However, he loves it. Therefore, I enjoy playing it with him. As a middle aged and non-athletic woman, I find myself sweating, running, and trying to dribble with my left hand. Why? Not because I like it, but because I want my son to know that I am interested in things that interest him.

For this same reason, I often find myself finger painting, morphing into a pretend Power Ranger, reading Doctor Zeus books, and learning how to properly throw a football. Each of these are activities I could stop doing and would not miss, but I do them often and frequently because my kids enjoy them.

What are some of the activities you have taken interest in solely because of your child? Fencing, cheering, piano, karate, debate or a favorite TV show? You may have had no previous interest in these activities but gained an interest solely because your child enjoyed it.

So it should be in marriage. You may not need to know how to restore an old car like he does, but stand over him and watch and learn. Learn the names of the tools and pass them to him as he asks. He will love it. Sit down on Sunday and watch a football game (As a side note here are two good tips that I learned about watching football with my man. 1. If you can only spare a little time then just watch the last half. 2. Save your questions for after the game or during commercials.) Your expressed interest and participation will say to him that you value spending time with him and you care about the things that make him uniquely him. When you accurately suggest that the center throw a flat snap and that the team move to a no-huddle offense because the clock is running down and they have no time outs left, he will look over at you as if you are sitting on the couch in red lingerie and heels!

I know some of you are saying "But he will never do any of the things that I like. So this is not fair." Remember, the plan of this book is to love better regardless of his responses, but be in prayer that he responds well. However, as a quick side note, a good tip to get him to enjoy some of your interests is to invite him to come along to the activities that are not as polarizing. Meaning, if you know he hates to shop, then do not invite him to the outlet mall with over 100 stores. Maybe just a trip to a specific department store for a specific item.

If you know he hates the theatre, don't take him to see Shakespeare. Consider inviting him to a non-chick-flick movie you may both enjoy.

Now, back to him. Ask him which of his hobbies or interests would he like you to participate in more. By participate, I mean his way. If he invites you into his world, don't judge it, critique it or belittle it. Just embrace it. Don't tell him that the game of football is too brutal and needs to be outlawed. Don't nag about how much money he spent restoring a car he rarely drives. Resist making a big deal about how smelly you all are after a fishing trip. Enhance the experience it, don't hinder it.

Remember, your involvement in the activity is not for the purpose of the activity itself. The goal is to get joy in sharing time with your mate, being invited into his space, and becoming your husband's friend.

*Wired for Fun*

Overall, men seem to be the gender that is more playful. Most often men will start the water fight when washing dishes or spontaneously stop for ice cream before eating dinner. As wives this type of behavior most often annoys us. Could it be because they were positioned to have more responsibility, God purposely gave them a childlike spirit to be able to "play out" (as opposed to working out) some of their stressors? Let's be mindful of the fact that this could be a God-given coping mechanism for men.

Are we working diligently to create memorable and joyous moments for our men? In the middle of a difficult business meeting, wouldn't it be great if your husband thought of the water gun fight you started this weekend. What if that thought was just what he needed to get through the rest of that meeting? Or when the thought of his mom's death sneaks up on him and makes him sad, what if the thought of you makes him laugh? Be the bright spot in your husband's day.

*Lighten Up*

Many times we focus on how much we have changed since getting married. Much of that focus is on the extra 20 pounds we've gained or the gray hairs that are starting to sprout. However, for most of us the greatest change is our sour and overly serious attitude. Even more damaging and unattractive than weight gain and grays, is negativity and boredom. Are you bringing any of these to your home?

Bobbing for Apples Again

One of my favorite months of the year is October. I love it. The temperature drops. I get to pull out my sweaters and my boots. The Texas State Fair rolls around and the thought of corn dogs, pineapple ice cream and funnel cakes overly excites me. I enjoy the preparations and decorations for autumn and Thanksgiving. I even get excited about the fun things associated with Halloween.

As I think about my best memories of Halloween, my thoughts drift to childhood. One of the activities that we did each year for Halloween was bob for apples. Kid after kid would immerse their faces in a huge bucket of water and apples, and see how many they could retrieve with their mouths in a certain timeframe.

Just thinking about this as an adult makes me want to gag. The once crystal clear water would swiftly become cloudy and discolored by face paint. The water that was once clean and pure would become a germ infested pool filled with half eaten popcorn kernels, hot dog bits, and saliva. I shudder at the thought!

As gross and unsanitary as this sounds, I don't remember any huge outbreaks of mono, strep, flu, or even colds following this event. What I do remember is how much fun we had. It was a blast and oftentimes the highlight of the Halloween event.

As my mature adult mind shudders at the thought of bobbing for apples, I wonder what other fun things I have educated my way out of. Where else has maturity won out against laughter and excitement? What things will I never do once or again because I'm just too informed and enlightened? Has your maturity affected your marriage? Does your husband see you as stiff, rigid, non-experimental and boring?

Do the responsibilities of being an adult often outweigh the excitement of life? Though there is great value in intelligence and maturity, they can co-exist with fun, excitement and laughter. So maybe all your life you have been told to "grow up!" and "act like a mature adult!" Well I am giving you permission to return to your childlike nature and go bobbing for apples in your marriage! Lighten up! Live a little!

In Matthew 19:14 Jesus said, "Let the little children come to me, and do not hinder them, for the kingdom of heaven belongs to such as these."

*Ramping Up the Routine*

I once read a book called *Losing your Marbles*. It was all about making the greatest impact on children's lives. One of the book's most impactful statements to me was that there is a secret of impact in the rhythms of life. That just by living life and in everyday moments, we create moments that matter.

Many times as wives, we get focused on the day's tasks, we lose sight of the day's rhythms. How do you make a car ride a bonding experience? Does your husband look forward to cuddling on the couch with you at night? Has the 15 minutes of one-on-one time while the coffee brews become a mandatory and meaningful ritual?

Marriage can become boring if we are not intentional about finding joy and fun in basic daily connections. Don't resent the routine. Revitalize it! Here are a few suggestions for making each day an experience:

- ❐ Stop living for the weekend. We have to stop viewing Monday through Thursday as doomsday and Friday evening as the day of Jubilee. I am not sure if you know this, but restaurants take reservations for 2 on Mondays. Parks are still open to the public on Tuesdays. Movies have showings on Thursdays. Fun activities do not have office hours. Stop "existing" through the week and "living" on weekends. Live life 7 days a week.

- Take daily selfies. I am not talking about photos either. Every day, do at least one thing that makes you and your husband smile. Go workout together every Tuesday night. Have a cheap date night at the coffee house nearby on Wednesday. This Thursday, call your girlfriend to babysit, while you and your husband go out for sushi. Whether 5 minutes or 50, take time for a daily selfie.

- Maximize the mundane. I have come to grips with the fact that my marriage does not exist in TV land. It's not always hysterical and dramatic. However, if I'm diligent to look, I can create and find wonderful moments.

- Shrink the "To Do" list. The weekday list of "To Dos" in most of our lives looks like rolling credits at the end of a movie. We spend our days trying to check off a list that is forever growing. If we overbook our days, then every day we will feel overbooked. If you are always so overbooked, then you will always be tired and irritable. Neither are healthy to marriage. Figure out what things are truly "must dos" and which things are "I'll get around tos."

- Change your thinking and your language. Don't refer to your job as "this stupid dump" but rather "the place that I get to showcase my talents and skills." Don't think of getting your kids ready in the morning and to school on time as the "morning rat race" but as "another moment to bond with your babies." Instead of saying "Monday *already?*" how about trying "Monday at last!" I know it may sound like the power of positive thinking—that's because it is. Your thinking changes your behavior and your behavior changes your experience. Make it a point to experience Monday differently this week and forever.

Ponder:

What are the specific interests of your husband? How have you enhanced or hindered these experiences? When was the last time you initiated a fun time with your husband? What was it? What was his response? Did you see any residual effect of that fun time?

Pray:

Lord, help me to lighten up and loosen up. God, give me the desire and authentic enjoyment of spending time with my husband doing the things that he likes to do.

Practice:

Do something spontaneous and fun with your husband today. Participate weekly in one of "his" activities with full acceptance. No nagging, questioning or remote sense of displeasure.

## FACEBOOK FUNNIES:

(posted by Eric) My wife and I are the best spades partners in the world! Any challengers? LOL!

— July 5, 2014

## CHAPTER 15 AND 1/2

# *Satan is a Hater*

*Then God said, "Let us make mankind in our image, in our likeness" So God created mankind in his own image, in the image of God he created them; male and female he created them. Genesis 1:26-27*

Why the ½? Because all the other issues fall under this main umbrella. The other issues are a symptom of this greater problem. If you get this one right, the others will fall in place like staggered dominos.

John 10:10 says, "The thief comes only to steal, kill and destroy." 1 Peter 5:8 further warns that "Your enemy, the devil, prowls like a roaring lion seeking someone to devour." Satan wants to destroy God and anything that represents Him.

The slang *hater* is a popular term used to refer to someone that wishes ill towards or is jealous of another. Haters often do things to intentionally derail the success of others. Satan is a hater.

He hates God. He hates those that love God. He hates you. He hates the institution designed by God to represent His love for us. Thus making marriage his primary target.

Through God's word, the bible, we get a detailed battle strategy to ward off Satan's attack. There is a bonus in the bible though! It is not only a battle strategy against Satan but it is also God's love letter to us. The bible is 2 testaments, 66 books, 1189 chapters and 31103 verses of wedding vows. Yes! God's proposal to us. We, the church, are His bride.

Satan understands the depth of the importance of successful marriages. Satan sees motherhood as an important battle but marriage as the essential war. Satan is attacking the source, the root, and the nucleus. It is the devil's specific plan to taint the beauty of marriage in order to taint the image of God's love for his people.

I have a friend who is an avid runner. Nearly every morning she will get up at the break of day and go for a run. One morning she noticed a gentleman taking a walk. It was a little strange that he was not in workout clothing. Instead, he wore denim pants and a plaid shirt. She did not think much of it. That is until she noticed him the next day, and the next and the next. Each day he walked her exact route and her exact time. Each morning getting closer to her. She then realized that this could be bad. She thought he could be watching her with the intent to one day rob, kidnap or even kill her.

She was upset with herself that it took her a week to realize she could be in danger. She admits that it was her naivety that caused her to be unaware and slow to act. Once she realized the impending danger, she attempted to get pictures of him. When he realized she was attempting to take his picture, he literally ran away. This sealed her speculation that this man was dangerous.

She alerted the police. She also changed the time, place and pattern of her runs. She was now fully aware that someone was out to harm her.

This awareness forced her to change her behaviors. Do not allow your naivety to dull your awareness of the truth that you have an enemy? You have an enemy that is watching and studying you. Studying your patterns. He knows your triggers, your fears, your insecurities and your weaknesses. He knows your husband's as well. So his full intent is to use these against you and to ultimately destroy your marriage.

Since we now understand that Satan has studied us and has picked apart our highlight reel of both good and bad footage, what is your strategy against him? Do you know your own weaknesses and triggers? What have you done to address, control and conquer them? What are your strengths and how have you maximized these in your marriage?

Have you taken a strengths inventory of your partner in battle? What makes him tick? What makes him blow? Where is he weak? What helps him function at his best?

There is a time to see your partner as your lover and your friend. However, you should never lose site of the reality that your husband is your combat partner. We have to spend less time fighting one another and more time fighting our adversary.

How ludicrous would this scenario be: Two American combat soldiers get into an argument with one another that is so intense it leads to a vicious battle. As they fight one another, the opposing army walks right up on them and slays them both. This happens daily in marriages!

Spouses are bickering over one party spending too much money on Christmas gifts. All the while Satan is setting up a financial unraveling that will lead to foreclosure and bankruptcy. Each blaming the other for the financial ruin.

Husbands and wives are in constant disagreement regarding discipline of the children. Satan, however, is thinking bigger. He is setting a plan in motion to lead your son into drugs and alcohol abuse, while mother and father hate each other for what the other one should have done to prevent this.

Couples are arguing about the extra weight the other has put on. While Satan is hatching a plan of deep betrayal and infidelity.

While you are spending exhaustive efforts on tiny battles, Satan is gunning for the war. Your husband is not your enemy, Satan is. Ephesians 6:12 says that "we wrestle not against flesh and blood, but against principalities, against powers, against the rulers of the darkness of this world, against spiritual wickedness in high places." Make sure you are fighting the true enemy!

Don't stop fighting! Don't let the hater have it, sister! Your commitment to your marriage is a direct testament to God's unconditional love for us. Fight for Christ by fighting for your marriage. This is a fight we can win.

*You are a soldier*

I love movies. My favorite are romantic comedies. My ideal Friday night would be laying on my couch with a bucket of buttery popcorn and a funny chick flick. Combat movies are much lower on my theater preference. I normally find my face peaking from behind my hands most of the movie. But there are many life and marital lessons to learn from war movies.

Most of these movies center around the relationship of fellow soldiers. The parallels that we can draw from these movies and apply to our marriage are staggering.

1. Building the bond: Soldiers leave their families behind and form a special and unbreakable bond with other soldiers. The reality of war connects them in a unique way. We must "leave and cleave" and "forsake all others" in order to establish a bond with our fellow solider in battle. This relationship will supersede all others.

2. Preparing for the battle: Training and preparation for soldiers is difficult and grueling. However, because of their intense preparation they are likely to defeat their opponent. As couples, we have to make sure that we are prepared for battle through consistent prayer, communication and connection.

3. Coming out together: Some of the most intense war movies draw us in with a scene during which one solider is determined to pull his wounded comrade to safety, never considering leav-

*Acing Motherhood But Failing Marriage*

ing him to die. How about you? When life deals your husband a hard blow, do you commit to pull him out of that season and to never leave him? Do you increase your compassion, your assistance, and commitment when he is not at his best? During the times when he is at this weakest, as his fellow comrade, fight for him. Don't leave him, emotionally or physically.

4. The victory celebration: After the war is won and they return home, the soldiers are normally greeted with a victory celebration. As you and your husband come out of difficult attacks launched on you by Satan, celebrate. Mark those moments of victory. Go to your favorite restaurant! Take a trip! Get intimate! Be intentional about celebrating the wins!

Ponder:

Reflect on the most difficult season in your marriage. What specific areas can you attribute to the strategic attack of Satan? In what specific ways did you and your husband fight for or against one another?

Pray:

Open my eyes to the spiritual realm. Give me wisdom, discernment and constant awareness of Satan's attack against my marriage.

Practice:

Celebrating! Identify a few situations that you and your spouse successfully fought through and won. Mark the moment with a celebration.

# FACEBOOK FUNNIES:

(posted by Eric) My wife is not respecting my NFL Sunday experience. She sits a load of clothes in front of me to fold. Please just go make me some Rotel and sit down!

— Football Season 2014

# *Conclusion*

A husband of one of my friends confessed in frustration to his wife that he often felt like a sperm donor. He went on to further express that he felt used, as if she got married just to have kids. Through their conversation he explained his dissatisfaction with feeling second, not prioritized and was embarrassed that he was jealous of his children.

Prior to reading this book you may have been quick to dismiss this as selfishness and immaturity. Hopefully by now though, you can agree that there is likely some validity to these emotions.

If you are not intentional about making your man your priority, you will treat him like the free gift at a fragrance counter. Oftentimes, especially near the holiday season, most department stores will offer some sort of free gift as a complement to your main fragrance purchase. Though the totes, after shaves and travel size samples are nice, that was not your chief acquisition.

Our children are the bonus gift set in life. Our husbands are the big bottle. Make it your mission to begin to think of and treat your husband as priority. As he begins to feel this shift, the dynamic of your relationship will shift as well.

Make a list of everything you would do for and with your husband if you did not have kids. After making that list, get to doing each and every one of those things. Some will be easy to accomplish. Others will take more coordination. Some will be short-term plans and others will be long-term visions. Working through this list will be a tangible technique to keep your relationship as wife and mother in proper balance.

What are you waiting for? Put this book down and get busy working your list!

www.ingramcontent.com/pod-product-compliance
Lightning Source LLC
Chambersburg PA
CBHW071313110426
42743CB00042B/1547